THE GREAT CANADIAN PRAIRIES BUCKET LIST

ROBIN ESROCK

ONE -OF-A- KIND TRAVEL EXPERIENCES

DUNDURN
TORONTO

This one's for Gary Kalmek

Library and Archives Canada Cataloguing in Publication

Esrock, Robin, 1974-, author
The great Canadian Prairies bucket list : one-of-a-kind travel experiences / Robin Esrock.

Issued in print and electronic formats.
ISBN 978-1-4597-3049-6 (paperback).--ISBN 978-1-4597-3050-2 (pdf).
-- ISBN 978-1-4597-3051-9 (epub)

1. Prairie Provinces--Guidebooks. 2. Esrock, Robin, 1974- --Travel--Prairie Provinces.
3. Prairie Provinces--Description and travel. I. Title.

FC3234.2.E86 2016   917.1204'4   C2015-908317-6
                                               C2015-908318-4

Editor: Allison Hirst
Cover and text concept: Tania Craan
Cover design: Courtney Horner
Text design: Laura Boyle
Front cover images: Chris Henderson Photography/Tourism Saskatchewan; Robin Esrock; Courtesy Canadian Museum for Human Rights; EWM; Joe Kalmek; thinkstock
Back cover images: (centre) Gary Kalmek; author photo, Neil Mumby/EWM
Printer: Friesens
1   2   3   4   5   20   19   18   17   16

We acknowledge the support of the **Canada Council for the Arts** and the **Ontario Arts Council** for our publishing program. We also acknowledge the financial support of the **Government of Canada** through the **Canada Book Fund** and **Livres Canada Books**, and the **Government of Ontario** through the **Ontario Book Publishing Tax Credit** and the **Ontario Media Development Corporation**.

Care has been taken to trace the ownership of copyright material used in this book. The author and the publisher welcome any information enabling them to rectify any references or credits in subsequent editions.   — *J. Kirk Howard, President*

The publisher is not responsible for websites or their content unless they are owned by the publisher.

Printed and bound in Canada.

Visit us at
Dundurn.com | @dundurnpress | Facebook.com/dundurnpress | Pinterest.com/dundurnpress

Dundurn
3 Church Street, Suite 500
Toronto, Ontario, Canada
M5E 1M2

CONTENTS

INTRODUCTION

bucket list: *A list of things one hopes to accomplish in one's lifetime.*

One fine spring morning, an unlicensed driver did not see a stop sign and barrelled across a downtown Vancouver intersection. This resulted in an unfortunate collision with a young man on a scooter heading up the road on his way to work. According to the crows, the young man executed an impressive swan dive, somersaulting over the delinquent vehicle to land like a sack of wheat. Judges would have scored it 10–9–10, if judges existed for such an event. As the young man in question, I can (rather gratefully) report that the mangled scooter in question never saw another road, and I lived to tell this tale in good health, give or take a broken kneecap.

The meaning of our lives can be deciphered in moments, and this accident — this moment — was indeed momentous. It was nothing less than life's alarm clock buzzing; a painful reminder that the destinations and activities I'd often dreamed of might never come to pass. Healed up and emboldened by a $20,000 insurance settlement, I quit my job and booked a solo twelve-month round-the-world ticket to visit twenty-four countries, and in the process, tick off my bucket list.

What started out as an adventure turned into an unexpected career. Pioneering a travel blog, I was soon writing about travel for major newspapers and magazines around the world, eventually hosting a National Geographic television series. Through it all, my job was to chase down exhilarating, one-of-a-kind experiences that belong on everybody's bucket list. My criteria were as follows:

- The experience must be unique in the world.
- It must be grounded in reality, so that can everyone actually do it.

- It must be an experience one will remember for the rest of one's life.
- Finally, the experience should make a great story at a dinner party, or in my particular case, for travel editors who have seen it all before.

If the activity or destination ticked off those very subjective boxes, I knew I'd found myself "one for the bucket list."

Writing a weekly travel column for the *Globe and Mail* newspaper, I took a hypothetical stab at Canadian experiences that met these criteria, too. Having visited more than one hundred countries on seven continents, I'd largely overlooked the amazing attractions of my adopted country, and it was time to rectify that situation. For the next three years, I visited every province and territory in search of the bucket list experiences that define our nation. In doing so, I uncovered not only incredible places and activities, but fascinating people and inspiring stories, too.

If most foreign visitors were to draw a map of Canada, it would contain Vancouver, the Rockies, Toronto, and Montreal. Saskatchewan and Manitoba would be lost in blank space, along with Atlantic Canada and the vast northern territories. This is hardly the fault of the tourism promotion folks, who do a fantastic job marketing the wonders of the region. It's just that Canada is so impossibly big, and beyond the major cities, only the Rockies are high enough to pierce the heavens of global tourism. This is unfortunate, but here's the good news: things are changing. Canadians, first of all, are realizing there's so much more to the Prairies than just wheat fields. With an increase in visitors from abroad, foreign tourists are noticing, too.

From the history of the Big Muddy Badlands to the wildlife wonders of Churchill, the Prairies are rich with adventures, culture, history, and a few quirks. Swim in Canada's own Dead Sea. Hook a giant catfish. Follow the underground footsteps of Al Capone. Let the hot breath of a polar bear fog up your camera! Repeated visits to the breadbasket provinces in both summer and winter allowed me to discover all this, and so much more. Who knew you could horseback ride with free-roaming plains bison, crack Canada's very own Da Vinci Code, or sunbathe on a powdery beach with sand more suited to the Caribbean? Isn't it time we celebrated the fact that the Prairies is the world's largest producer of mustard seed, or that each year one of the largest number of vertebrate species in the world gathers here?

Although you may have found this book in the travel section, you'll quickly realize it's not a traditional guidebook. Rather than focusing on prices and meal recommendations — many of which will change before this book even goes to print — I've focused on why you should visit these destinations in the first place. It is a personal journey, rife with context and characters, humour and history. Suitably inspired, I want you to follow in my footsteps (in order to make your own). That's why I've created a comprehensive website with all the information you'll need to get started. At the end of each chapter, follow the website link to find practical information, links, meal and accommodation recommendations, videos, galleries, maps, and suggested reading guides. You'll also find regular blog updates, tips, and commentary, and a chance to share your own experiences. Up-to-date information might be great online, but inspiration has always worked wonders on the printed (or digital) page.

One might argue that every provincial park, historic site, city, or museum belongs on the Canadian Prairies Bucket List, and they would be right. In these pages you will find some obvious choices, and you may notice some terrible omissions, some head-scratching facts, and hopefully a few laughs, too. It's an honour to be your guide, and it is a role I take seriously (although not too seriously, because if there's one thing I've learned from travelling in Canada, it's how to laugh in the face of adversity).

There are so many people to meet and so many bucket list adventures to discover. I needed an accident to remind me it was time to start living. All you need to do is turn the page.

Robin Esrock
Vancouver, B.C.

* *"The Prairies" often refers to the provinces of Alberta, Saskatchewan, and Manitoba. Since Alberta features in the Western Canada edition of this series, this book only covers Saskatchewan and Manitoba.*

HOW TO USE THIS BOOK

You will notice this bucket list includes little information about prices, where to stay, where to eat, the best time to go, and what you should pack. Important stuff, but these are practicalities that shift and change with far more regularity than print editions of a book. With this in mind, I've created online and social media channels to accompany the inspirational guide you hold in your hands. Here you will find practical information, along with videos, galleries, reading suggestions, and more.

By visiting www.canadianbucketlist.com, you can also join our community of Bucket Listers, with exclusive discounts to many of the activities featured in this book, automatic entry to win experiences featured in the book, as well as Facebook forums to debate the merits of these, and new adventures. When you register, you can unlock the entire site by entering the code BUCK3TL15T and navigating through the provinces, or access each item individually with the START HERE link at the end of each chapter.

DISCLAIMER

Tourism is a constantly changing business. Hotels may change names, restaurants may change owners, and some activities may no longer be available at all. Records fall and facts shift. While the utmost care has been taken to ensure the information provided is accurate, the author and publisher take no responsibility for errors, or for any incidents that might occur in your pursuit of these activities.

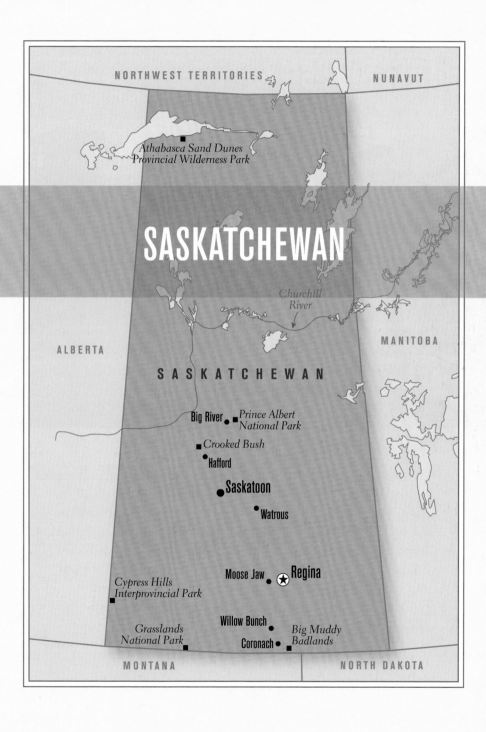

SALUTE THE RCMP

The red serge is such a Canadian icon that the Mounties have trademarked it. After all, this is a police force on which others around the world are modelled. I want to understand just what the Royal Canadian Mounted Police is, who these people are, and what makes them so great. I want to chase cars and shoot guns and catch bad guys. I want to *be* RCMP. So it's off to Regina's Depot, the very soul of the RCMP, the mother from which all cadets are birthed.

The excellent Arthur Erickson–designed Heritage Museum can answer my questions, but I want to get inside the organization's skin. So I continue driving, through the security gate, warned that I might encounter live training exercises. At the clothing facility, the Stores Person, Sean Lussier, measures me up: I am freckled, accented, with a streak of anti-authority tendencies. Mind you, he's got tattoos, piercings, and a waxed moustache. Sean pulls out his pencil and tape measure. I am fitted with formal and casual wear and handed a pair of leather boots that need to be polished for twenty-five hours before they attain the appropriate sheen. He tells me new cadets tear up when they try on the red serge for the first time. I slip on the red blazer and immediately feel three inches taller.

It's off to the barber, where, from a selection of short, shorter, and eight ball, I really begin to look the part. In the morning I am taking the Physical Ability Requirement Evaluation (PARE), an obstacle designed to challenge the bodies and minds of incoming cadets. New cadets must complete four circuits of the course in under 4:45, plus tackle a weight mechanism. If they fail, they are given three days to give it another go. Failing that, they are released from duty, dreams and all. To graduate, the PARE must be completed within four minutes.

Cadets sleep on average just five hours a night. They will pack in the studies equivalent to a four-year degree in just twenty-six weeks. Speaking to some of them at breakfast in the canteen, I learn just how determined they are to make it, and how proud they are to be RCMP. I eat lightly before nervously making my way to the gym for the PARE test. Prior to the attempt, each cadet's blood pressure is checked as a precaution, which only succeeds in rocketing the nerves.

I am shown how to jump over this, hop over that, up the stairs, around the orange cone, on my back, on my front, again, again, again. The clock starts, and I keep an even pace. It doesn't seem too difficult at first. By the second lap, I am breathing heavily. Cadets are starting to cheer. By the third lap, my body feels ambushed. The jumps seem longer, my steps heavier. Fourth lap, the cadets are cheering, "Go Robin!" I can't let them down. If they see me fail, they'll be discouraged, and here is a room full of future peace officers, people who will save lives. I'm choking for lack of breath but continue to the weight machine, where I must thrust my body forward and pull weights in a fluid semicircle. My heart tries to rip itself out like the creature in

They Always Get Their Man

- The RCMP is the provincial police force for all provinces except Quebec, Ontario, and Newfoundland and Labrador. It provides additional policing services to two hundred municipalities in Canada and nearly two hundred First Nations communities.
- The red serge, which is worn only at civic ceremonies, celebrations, and memorials, consists of a scarlet tunic with a low-neck collar and brass buttons. The pants are black riding breeches with a yellow stripe down each leg. Spurs accompany brown leather riding boots.
- The Dempster Highway was named after RCMP inspector William John Dempster, for his service to the North.
- Charles Dickens's son served as a member of the North-West Mounted Police, a precursor to the RCMP.
- Women first graduated as RCMP members in March 1975.
- The last RCMP dog patrol was in 1969.
- The RCMP served in the Boer War, and the First and Second World Wars.
- Only Canadian citizens can join the RCMP.
- There are currently over 27,000 members and employees of the RCMP. ➤

Alien. Still, the cadets are cheering, and their cheering keeps me going. Suddenly I understand why home ice is so important.

I complete the task and pick up a thirty-six-kilogram bag, carefully carrying it around a cone and returning it in complete control. The sergeant announces my time: 3:50. I collapse in exhaustion, the cadets cheering. Already they are beginning their rotations, so I am whisked out of the gym. Who needs media at a time like this? Corporal Dan, the communications officer showing me around, is impressed. I'm coughing up intestine, tasting the iron of blood at the back of my throat. "That's the PARE cough," says the corporal. "You'll have it for a couple days."

No time to recover. I rush off to formation marching and the daily Sergeant Major's Parade, where I am picked on by a mean-looking corporal, who makes me fully aware of his garlic-heavy diet. Cadets stand to attention as stiff as a pine forest. Then it's off to the Police Driving Unit, where Corporal Darcy Jacksteit allows me to join him

for the day's exams. We play out various scenarios in his Crown Victoria, as I learn about RCMP policies and just how stressful it can be behind the wheel. After some evasive-driving procedures, I'm dropped off at a firearms unit, learning that guns are the last-ditch attempt and should always be aimed for maximum impact. Cadets will spend a minimum of fifty-two hours at the range.

Finally, I visit Sergeant B.J. Landry's Simulator Training Unit, where high-tech cameras and simulators allow me to play out life-and-death scenarios in safety but under scrutiny. Police forces from around the world train at the Depot, sometimes employing RCMP policies. No other country has a national police force charged with performing so many roles — from policing to drug enforcement, immigration and borders to terrorism. A movie made the maxim famous: "The Mountie always gets his man." This, unfortunately, is not always the case. Yet, despite the clobbering the organization gets in the news media, its standards and traditions are of the highest calibre.

Growing up in South Africa, we were afraid of police. They were very often just as crooked as the thieves they were supposed to catch. Not so in Canada. It might not be on everyone's bucket list to put themselves through a crash course of cadet training. Yet everyone needs to visit the Heritage Museum and learn about this vital Canadian institution — to try on the red serge and see how it fits.

START HERE: canadianbucketlist.com/rcmp

CLIMB CASTLE BUTTE IN BIG MUDDY

Scramming from Regina south on a straight-as-a-church-choir highway, we're leaving the RCMP in the dust in search of the Big Muddy Badlands. It is a region famed for its outlaws, and it's their spirit I blame for flooring a rental car that growls its distaste for the one-hundred-kilometre speed limit. Like many highways in Saskatchewan, this one seems purposely built for land speed records. Turning left onto SK-36, the smooth highway becomes cratered and cracked, as if an attacking squadron of fighter jets has strafed it.

"How do you like our road?" asks the lady at Coronach's Co-op pump, clearly unimpressed with the provincial Highway Commission. By the time you read this, we're all hoping the road to Coronach is as smooth as the gravel country roads that surround it. Either way, it all adds to the adventure of seeking out a place where tumbleweed is blown by the ghostly breaths of lawlessness. For a while, the Big Muddy Badlands epitomized the Wild West, where rustlers eluded pursuing posses and rogue outlaws demonstrated the charm and gunmanship touted in nineteenth-century romance novels. Even today, you can hear the sound of six-shooters whistling in the strong prairie breeze.

"Oh, people visit us from around world," explains Big Muddy's welcoming guide Trish Manske. We pick her up at the modest Coronach Visitor Centre, from which daily summer tours to the Badlands depart. Trish has lived on a ranch nearby for decades, and she's eager to show us why Big Muddy belongs on every Canadian's bucket list. Van tours take place in July and August, but we're here for a private tour in spring. The Long Tour is a 180-kilometre round trip to visit eight separate sites. A ninth could be added if you factor in the scenery. For while the drive to Coronach was one of flat and endless wheat fields, once we enter the valley, fields drop into sandstone valleys, buttes of elephant skin–like sedimentary rock rise from the valley floor, recalling glacial action some 65 million years ago. Thousands of bison once feasted on the valley's grassland, supporting numerous First Nation tribes. Neither survived the influx of European hunters and ranchers.

Located within sight of the Montana border, this is where the Land of the Living Skies (Saskatchewan) meets Big Sky Country (Montana). Running along this porous international border is a fence, although

word on the prairie is that some rocks are actually hidden cameras and drones patrol overhead. Our first stop is the valley's most striking natural landmark, Castle Butte. Think of it as Canada's Ayers Rock. Jutting sixty metres out of the valley like a camel's hump, it is five hundred metres in circumference and offers those brave enough to climb up an outstanding view of the surrounding valley. Aboriginal people used it as a vantage point to spot bison herds roaming the plains. The Northwest Mounted Police used it to spot outlaws.

"Can I climb it?" I ask Trish.

"That's what it's for," she replies.

You can't do that at Ayers Rock.

It's a quick scramble to the top. Eroding sandstone provides plenty of footholds up the steep banks, although I'm a little nervous about the sinkholes, some of which are the size of manhole covers, and deep as a well. The brisk prairie wind is howling, the fifty-five-kilometre valley stretches below. Legend has it that when the glaciers melted, one could paddle from Big Muddy all the way to the Gulf of Mexico. No one was around with a canoe back then, but by the late 1800s, ranchers had settled throughout the valley. Far removed from the reach of the Northwest Mountain Police (the forebears of today's RCMP), Big Muddy attracted a different sort of settler.

"Dutch Henry was the ring leader," explains Tamela Burgess, matriarch of the eight-thousand-hectare Burgess Ranch. Tammy has become the go-to Badlands historian, penning a book about the bandits, tracing photographs, researching tales long buried in the dust. She's built an outlaw gallery on her ranch, the same ranch that hosted the first detachment of mounted police in 1902. She has drawn portraits of Big Muddy's principal characters — the ranchers, the law, and most intriguingly, the outlaws. It didn't take long for smooth-talking, likeable horse wranglers to see the thieving potential of the Badlands. Not only would the international border deter chasing posses, but the region's caves provided natural hideouts for both men and horses. This is why *Butch Cassidy and the Sundance Kid*, immortalized by Paul Newman and Robert Redford in the film of the same name, chose Big Muddy as Station One in an outlaw trail that stretched all the way from Canada to Mexico. A station might consist of a friendly (or fearful) rancher who would provide shelter and food, or a hideout safe from the pursuing law. Dutch Henry's "Wild Bunch" would steal horses from the United States and rebrand them to be sold to Canadian ranchers. If Canadian ranchers thought they were getting a good deal, they underestimated the cunning of the gang. Their own horses would be stolen and re-branded for another cross-border swap. The Wild Bunch was even known to sell stolen horses back to their original owners. Integral to the scheme were co-operative ranchers, and integral to this co-operation was an atmosphere of fear. This is where notorious thugs like Sam Kelly and Bloody Knife came in; dead-eyed men with reptilian blood and a thirst for violence. They even murdered one of their own — a fellow outlaw who botched a train job south of the border. Legend holds that Sam Kelly dehorned a steer with his rifle from one hundred metres away, although an old photograph in the gallery depicts him as boyish beyond his years. Tammy eagerly shares the stories of these and other characters, explaining how the intimidated ranchers finally stood up for themselves, and the positive impact on

the area when Big Muddy at last received a full Mountie detachment. Ironically, Sam Kelly never went to jail, and lived out his days in the region. Various theories abound about the fate of Dutch Henry, an enigmatic character begging for the Hollywood treatment. Tammy's portrait of Henry makes him look like a 1970s-era Burt Reynolds.

We leave the Burgess Ranch with a real feel for the characters that put the *bad* in *badlands*, and an appreciation for Tammy's enthusiasm to share their stories with visitors each summer.

A few miles away, Trish unlocks and swings open a heavy gate. We drive along a natural spring to find a sign boldly revealing the twin Sam Kelly Outlaw Caves. One was for the men, the other for the contraband horses. Adjacent is a pyramid-like hill that provided an ideal lookout for police or posses. The caves have been restored with wood beams, but there's not much more to them than holes in a hill. It's not hard to imagine the cowboys, whittling away on branches, rolling tobacco in stony silence. Now the tour veers toward the artifacts left behind by the First Nations who once hunted bison in the valley, including an eighteen-metre-wide stone circle, and bison and turtle effigies. The origin of these effigies remains a mystery, but the

The Giant of Willow Bunch

Highway 13, on the way to Coronach, passes through a small community called Willow Bunch, which at one time happened to be the home of Canada's tallest man. Edouard Beaupré was born in 1881, and, before the age of nine, he stood six feet in height. Due to abnormal amounts of natural growth hormones, Eduoard eventually towered over his peers at seven feet eight inches. By all accounts a gentle giant, Edouard toured North America as a circus freak and strongman to earn income for his family (he would raise large horses on his shoulders). He died of tuberculosis when he was just twenty-three while working for the Ringling Bros Circus at the 1904 St. Louis World Fair. For decades, his mummified remains remained at the University of Montreal, until they were finally returned to his hometown in 1990, where they were cremated and laid to rest outside a museum that continues to honour the Giant of Willow Bunch. ➤

views across the valley from here are astounding. The Long Tour takes in the Heritage School House, the Big Beaver Nature Centre, and Aust's General Store ("If we don't have it, you don't need it.") A shorter half-day tour takes in the highlights. Infused with the landscape are the stories. We know the Sundance Kid sent postcards from Big Muddy (there's no evidence that Butch Cassidy was in the area, although everyone believes it was highly likely). We know that the rancher who hosted the first NWMP detachment was in the pocket of the Wild Bunch, and re-branded the stolen horses right under the noses of the law. We know about the Mountie's wife who rustled horses on the side. Beyond these terrific stories, it's the landscape that leaves the biggest impression. Stories of law and order forever at odds in the badlands of Saskatchewan.

START HERE: canadianbucketlist.com/bigmuddy

BUST THE CHICAGO CONNECTION

Visiting Saskatchewan can feel like a game of cops and robbers. We visited outlaw caves in Big Muddy, put on the Red Serge at the RCMP Depot, and now we've taken a forty-five-minute drive west of Regina to Moose Jaw in order to get our gangster on, *capisci*? For most of the century, Moose Jaw authorities denied the existence of an underground labyrinth beneath the buildings on the city's Main Street. After all, nobody is fond of revealing skeletons in closets located in secret rooms. Unless, of course, those skeletons can intrigue tourists, in which case, bring out the bone polish!

The Tunnels of Moose Jaw recreates the city's infamous history with two fifty-minute underground tours exploring Chinese immigration in the early twentieth century ("Passage to Fortune") and the

role Moose Jaw played during the Prohibition years ("The Chicago Connection"). Renovated to recall both periods, re-enactors lead us through passageways and hidden rooms, explaining how the tunnels were used — first as access corridors for steam engineers, then as a safe haven for Chinese migrants fearing for their lives, and finally by bootleggers and gangsters. Although there's no physical evidence he ever visited "Chicago North," Al Capone's ghost is everywhere here. Gangster history of that era is soaked in rum, myth, and hearsay. What is known for certain is that Moose Jaw was an important distribution centre for rumrunners smuggling booze into the United States on CPR's Soo Line. During this period, local law enforcement consisted of a Chief of Police by the name of Walter P. Johnson, a man firmly in the pocket of the gangsters. In exchange for peace and envelopes stuffed with cash, Capone's men essentially had the run of the town, operating gambling, booze, and prostitution rings in the refashioned tunnels, safe from prying eyes. When prohibition ended, the tunnels were abandoned, their existence either denied or forgotten. That is, until their reopening in 2000 as a lively historical tourist attraction.

At the entrance on Main Street, old newspaper clippings and exhibits immediately set the tone for an underground adventure that takes visitors back in time into the city's seedy past. Two re-enactors lead us across the street to where the tour will begin. We enter a saloon to the sounds of honky-tonk piano. Our guide, Miss Fanny, a vivacious lady of dubious profession, sets the mood. It is 1927, an era of temperance. Alcohol has been outlawed in the United States, creating rich opportunities for Canadian liquor operations close to the border. Speakeasies are doing a roaring trade, but the fear of police and FBI raids permeate the air along with cheap perfume and cotton-wool clouds of cigarette smoke. Even with the law in their pockets, for gangsters on the lam, the tunnels of Moose Jaw are the perfect place to operate. We walk down a narrow staircase, Miss Fanny passing us off to a young Wise Guy with a thick "Joisey" accent. He shows us where the boys gambled, sent and received radio communications, hoarded booze, and stockpiled their Thomson sub-machine guns, all the while reminding us to "forgeddaboutit!"

It's fun and hammy, and the entire time I'm thinking, "Really, this is happening each day beneath the streets of downtown Moose Jaw?" By the end of the tour, I'm pulling my hat low and my collar up. Walking onto Main Street, there's a jarring feeling when we return to the present, to our own era of law and order. Although the truth was probably less glamorous, Moose Jaw's gangster history smuggles itself onto the Prairies Bucket List. No questions about it, *capisci?*

START HERE: canadianbucketlist.com/moosejaw

SUPPORT RIDER NATION

The first time I heard the word *Roughriders*, I thought it was a brand of condoms. Immigrants to Canada have to face these sorts of challenges, such as how to pronounce *Saskatchewan*, or follow the puck, or learn to believe that a place called Moose Jaw actually exists. It took me some time to understand that Canadian football is different from American football, and that the most rabid fans in the CFL, if not the country, belong to Regina's own Roughriders. Indeed, when you visit

Why the Watermelons?

Visitors to a Roughriders game will notice the colour green, lots of beer, and people with watermelons on their heads. This is especially strange, because watermelons don't grow in Saskatchewan, and can be hard to find when the season extends into the cold months of October and November. Ask five fans why they're wearing watermelons and you'll get six answers, and a cold beer. Some believe it's a statement that the Roughriders are so good they can wear fruity helmets for protection. Some believe it's because they're cheap to buy and fun to carve. There's a legend of some local students inventing the craze, and another that claims placing sticky watermelons on the head is the perfect way to cool down on a hot summer day. My research led me to someone else's research, which told of a couple of kids who went to Winnipeg to support the Riders in 2001, covered themselves in green, and capped it off with a watermelon. Their antics attracted local media, which in turn attracted the marketing department of the Roughriders, who promptly encouraged the fashion, much to the delight of local watermelon suppliers. This may or may not be the winning theory, but when it comes to supporting Rider Nation, results rarely count for much anyway. ➤

Saskatchewan, you are actually visiting Rider Nation, where you'll no doubt get swept up in a frenzy of Rider Pride. This is why it's really important you don't tell anyone you once thought Roughriders was a brand of condoms. They might just stick a watermelon on your head.

It's game day for the Riders. Even though they didn't qualify for this year's Grey Cup playoffs, the fans are ready to brave sub-zero temperatures to show their enthusiastic support for the team. The Riders are far from the most successful team in the CFL (they've only won a handful of trophies after more than one hundred years of chasing the ball), but fans of Canada's biggest sports franchises have a high threshold for failure. I'm throwing myself into the mix, donning the Green and White, painting my face, applying temporary Rider tattoos, putting on green bug glasses and a bright green wig. Covering it all is a thick jacket; otherwise, all the swag will freeze to my skin. Initially I thought I'd overdone it, but as I walk from the Hotel Saskatchewan to Mosaic Stadium, I am snug among the faithful.

I ask some locals to explain the passion for the Riders. "Well, we haven't got a heck of a lot going on besides the Riders," says one chap. "They're the best thing we got going!" yells another, and I begin to sense a theme. Without a hockey franchise, Saskatchewan only has one team to represent the province in the media limelight, and come snow or freezing rain, they're going to support them every yard of the way.

It's the last game of the season, and a game of meaningless consequence. The opponents are the Hamilton Tiger-Cats, who sound like characters from a Saturday morning cartoon. It's my first ever CFL game, and a real glimpse into a Canadian sport determined to differentiate itself from the strikingly similar, much more popular version of the game just south of the border. Canadian fields are larger, the team has one extra player, there are only three downs instead of four, and the game has all sorts of strategic, tactical, and rule differences. For a newbie like myself, both sports provide an opportunity to watch large armoured men slam into each other while pretty young girls with pompoms do backflips — therefore, a grand day out, whatever side of the border you happen to be on. I take my seat and immediately scream "Go Riders!" at the top of my lungs. I probably should have waited until they finished singing the national anthem.

Mosaic Stadium holds thirty thousand people and is neither covered nor heated. This is important to note should the playoffs extend into November, when Regina has recorded temperatures as low as –37°C. If you can survive watching a football game when the thermometer retreats well below zero, you deserve to support the best team in the entire universe, of any sport, period.

As the game proceeds, I do as the locals do: yell at the visitors ("Tiger-Cats, more like Pussy-Cats!"), yell at the referee ("I don't know what rules you're following, but only Riders rule!"), crack open hand warmers in my pockets, and drink copious amounts of beer. This endears me to fellow fans, and I receive not one but two fluffy key chain toys of Gainer, the Riders' lovable gopher mascot. I am told Gainer pioneered the art of beating stuffed lions and tigers in the middle of a football field.

After an awful season, and against all odds, the Riders emerge triumphant, providing some consolation for Canada's most festive fans. Another season is over, but there's always next year, when the mighty Riders will charge for the Cup yet again. Time your visit to Regina to coincide with a game and you'll see why Rider Pride scores a touchdown on the Prairies Bucket List.

START HERE: canadianbucketlist.com/riders

FLOAT IN CANADA'S DEAD SEA

Before you die, you really should experience the wonders of the Dead Sea. With its banks being the lowest place on dry land on Earth, and with waters 8.6 times saltier than the ocean, one floats without any effort, cradled by the lifeless yet legendary therapeutic waters. The Dead Sea splits Israel and Jordan in the Middle East, which is a little far to travel even by Canadian standards. So it's Saskatchewan to the rescue, with its own lake, unique in the western hemisphere, located just a ninety-minute drive southeast of Saskatoon.

Twelve thousand years ago, a receding glacier trapped a lake at the bottom of a valley. Hemmed in by the valley walls, water was prevented from seeping away by pressure caused by groundwater aquifers. Thousands of years of evaporation later, the result is Little Manitou Lake, with waters three times saltier than the ocean and laced with all sorts of wonderfully helpful minerals. As in the Dead Sea, you can float, you can heal, and you can smother yourself in goopy mud that international spas could market for small fortunes.

Having visited the Dead Sea a number of times, I admit I am skeptical. Surely, if such a lake existed, it would be on the world map, or at least North America's. Driving through the prairie, passing small towns and potash mines, I have a sinking feeling (ahem) that Little Manitou will not live up to the hype. Although few people outside the area know about it today, it was immensely popular in the 1950s. "Canada's Carlsbad!" reads an enthusiastic wooden sign as I enter Watrous, the nearest town. It's sleepy and quiet, but then again, so are the towns that service the Dead Sea. I check into the Manitou Springs Hotel and Spa, my room offering a lovely view of the calm lake mirroring a big prairie sky. A few people are taking a dip, but nobody is floating on their back. Downstairs, the "rich golden colour" of the heated indoor mineral pools looks suspiciously like dirty tea, even if it is 100 percent natural.

I walk across the street to find adults sunbathing among rows of kids playing on the coarse sandy beach. I try to imagine Cree Indians on these same banks, discovering, to their surprise, that drinking and bathing in the water cured deathly fevers and painful rheumatism. Legend has it a group of sick men were left for dead here, only to recover thanks to the water's healing properties. When they returned to their tribe, they were initially thought to be ghosts.

Chemically, the water is rich: magnesium (helps regulate body temperature, tones skin); potassium (antibacterial); sulphate (aids nervous, blood, muscular, and lymph systems); calcium (great for the skin); silica (skin tone, bone and nail growth); sulphur (for aching joints and collagen synthesis) — all of which should easily take care of the uric acid, as contributed by the small kids playing in the shallow areas. Unlike the suitably named Dead Sea, there is life in these waters: brine shrimp, bugs, and a sticky green weed the kids are collecting to make messy wigs.

I walk to the edge, dip in my toe-thermometer, lie back, and expect to sink like a stone. Instead, the water makes me buoyant, and I find myself easily floating on my back. Admittedly, the liquid is not as supportive as the Dead Sea, but it's comfortable enough, in that one would have to work very hard to drown oneself. After applying and rinsing off the mud, I find my skin wonderfully silky and shiny, making me wonder why Dead Sea mud sells for big bucks while Manitou mud is unheard of. Watrous, there's cash to be made here! The Dead Sea undoubtedly benefits from that repetitive Trio of Important Rules: location, location, location. Manitou, on the other hand, literally means "Great Spirit" in Cree, a godly lake blessed with healing, recreational, and definite bucket list qualities.

START HERE: canadianbucketlist.com/manitou

Hot Pools in Moose Jaw

In 1910, oil drillers accidentally discovered a source of geothermal water in Moose Jaw, much to the delight of all the aching backs in the province. A new well was drilled in the 1980s, which today feeds water through an insulated pipeline to the luxury Temple Gardens Hotel and Spa. Rich in minerals similar to those found in the spas in Bath, England, the indoor and outdoor pools are located in downtown Moose Jaw, which claims to offer the most attractions per capita in Canada. ➤

VISIT A HAUNTED GROVE

Peering out a window of the landmark Delta Hotel Bessborough in Saskatoon, watching traffic cross a stone bridge over the idyllic South Saskatchewan River, I thought I'd been transplanted to Europe. A half-hour later, in my rental car, the city dissipates into a string of strip malls, homesteads, farmsteads, and finally no steads at all, just endless flat fields of wheat. An ominous sky hovers above the autumn chill. My destination is a mysterious grove of deformed aspen trees that locals believe might be the freakiest trees in all of Canada. It begs investigation and provides a neat excuse to drive north into the prairie to see for myself. Crooked Bush is not on any maps. Once I drive through the small town of Hafford, I stop and ask for directions at a gas station. It looks as if it could easily be the location for the hit Canadian sitcom *Corner Gas*. Fortunately, the pimply kid behind the counter knows exactly what I'm looking for. Apparently "Y'all ain't the first stranger driving these parts lookin' for trees."

He hands me a one-page sheet containing information about Crooked Bush. "The Crooked Bush is a group of wild aspen trees that … twist, loop, and bend into the eeriest of forests. Courage of stone is necessary to visit it at night." Fortunately, I've planned my visit during the day, although I score extra points for making it the week of Halloween. With no help from the pamphlet's awfully confusing directions, I get lost within ten minutes of turning off the highway. When in doubt, follow those in front of you. I hope the pickup truck in question is also seeking the strange and unusual, and not, say, a tractor part. Ten minutes later, a lopsided wooden sign, written in what can best be described as witch scrawl, points right. A small clearing leads to a wooden boardwalk with a sign boldly proclaiming I've arrived at a legendary botanical mystery.

Exiting the car, hunched up against the cold, I take a few steps, stop, and start yelling into the bitter wind. "Tim! Tim? Are you there?" Only director Tim Burton's warped mind could possibly have created the trees that knot themselves over the boardwalk: silver-flecked branches with black scars, tangled and twisted, like the claws of a goblin, or the dislocated legs of a giant spider. While university researchers have determined that some form of genetic mutation causes the trees to grow as they do, mystery still surrounds what led to the mutation in the first place, and why forests of perfectly normal, straight aspen trees surround the grove. Locals in the area have claimed to see UFOs, while others point fingers at meteorites, contaminated soil, or overzealous imaginations. My favourite theory belongs to the farmer who claims to have seen an alien urinate in the area before the trees began to grow in the 1940s. This might explain another creepy forest in Poland, where pine trees are deformed at ninety-degree angles. After all, even little green men gotta go when they gotta go.

Spooks in Saskatchewan

1. The St. Louis Ghost Train is a steady white glow followed by a red light, a mysterious oncoming locomotive that never arrives. While some believe it to be car lights, local legend attributes the ghostly lights to a decapitated conductor.

2. In 1938, a mysterious bouncing light startled a resident walking through the Tabor Cemetery near the town of Esterhazy. Accompanied by a chill in the air, other residents saw it, too, and soon enough, the Tabor lights captured the nation's attention.

3. Haunting the abandoned mines between the towns of Bienfait and Estevan are the *rugaroos* — mean-mannered, shape-shifting ancient Native spirits with glowing red eyes and a penchant for mischief.

4. The community of Brickleigh was notoriously haunted for half a century, until the 1980s, when a farmer unearthed a human skull. It is thought to have belonged to a murdered railwayman, whose ghost has since been quiet.

5. Fleeing a Blackfoot raiding party, three Assiniboine women are said to have drowned in Old Wives Lake. On calm days, locals claim they can still hear screaming across the water.

6. An elderly female ghost, said to be the kindly spirit of a former nurse, haunts the hallways of Regina General Hospital. Meanwhile, the ghost of Howie, a cook who died in the mansion in the 1930s, is said to haunt Government House. ➤

The boardwalk is not very long, and there are a few standout rock star trees that hog attention. Another couple arrive, telling me they'd heard about the trees for years. On Halloween, the Gothically inclined are known to throw creepy parties here, and they're welcome to it. There's definitely something strange in the air, an energy charged by aliens, meteors, or an arboreal sense of humour. The chill is piercing my fleece, and Mrs. Esrock has run back to the car to catch up with her imagination. A few minutes later I join her for the return drive to Saskatoon, as the late-afternoon sun peeks out from under the clouds, brightening up the wheat fields. The drive is straight, long, and unmistakably beautiful. No verdict on

whether Crooked Bush is, in fact, one of the most haunted spots in Canada. But for providing an excuse to drive into the prairie on a fun, hare-brained adventure, it deserves its spot on the Prairies Bucket List.

START HERE: canadianbucketlist.com/crookedbush

STARGAZE IN A DARK SKY PRESERVE

Many years ago, human beings navigated their past, present, and future by the stars. The movement of these celestial bodies determined the seasons and festivals, the direction in which to point foot, wagon, or ship. Constellations gave birth to the mythology of gods, immortalized in pinpricks of light in the darkest of skies.

For those of us living in cities, it's a rare night indeed when we can observe the full glory of space. *Sky glow* is a term used for powerful urban light sources that surround a city — from the street lights, buildings, and stadiums. It creates an orange haze scattered by reflections in the dust, airbrushing out the darkness of night. We don't see the Milky Way, the movement of planets and constellations,

SASKATCHEWAN

the nightly reminder of how little we know and how small our problems really are. This light pollution protects us from ourselves, a comforting blanket to warm us against the chill of insignificance. It is also an illuminated bandit that robs us of a view that is, literally, out of this world.

Fortunately, Canada is a country that leads the way in the creation of Dark Sky Preserves, areas protected from artificial light, promoting astronomy while allowing for the study of darkness's impact on wildlife. As of this writing, Canada has twenty of the forty-nine Dark Sky Preserves that have been established worldwide, and the tightest controls to ensure they remain true refuges of night. Saskatchewan has two Dark Sky Preserves: the Cypress Hills Interprovincial Park it shares with Alberta, and the nine-hundred-square-kilometre Grasslands National Park.

Grasslands is Canada's darkest Dark Sky Preserve and has the highest rating on the Bortle Dark Sky Scale, a nine-level Richter-like measure for nocturnal darkness. Here you can see faint traces of the earth's airglow, the weak emission of planetary light, while parts of the Milky Way actually cast shadows on the ground. Parks Canada holds free stargazing events, guided by astronomers from the Royal Astronomical Society of Canada. High-powered telescopes are available to the public. So clear are the stars that you can see the Triangulum Galaxy with the naked eye, a galaxy three million light years away. Even a pair of binoculars will serve as an able telescope. The best place to view the stars in the park's West Block is at the Belza Viewpoint, or the Two Tree Trail Access Road. McGowan's Campground and Dawson's Viewpoint are ideal in the East Block.

It took a while for my eyes to adjust, and for the sheer spectacle of the night sky to manifest itself. Satellites and shooting stars are abundant, almost overwhelming. Lying down, wrapped warm in a blanket, I have to remind myself this isn't a planetarium, but that I'm perfectly safe to enjoy the dark dome above me, exposed and

Starbathing in the City

If you can't get to a Dark Sky Preserve, visit the University of Saskatchewan's Campus Observatory in Saskatoon. Each clear Saturday night, the observatory focuses its three-metre refracting telescope on planets, clusters, galaxies, and the occasional unsuspecting comet. Admission is free. ➤

vulnerable on the soft prairie grassland. When it's time to leave, I check the time on my cellphone and the backlight stings my retina. Rays of car beams cause me to squint. Slowly I reacquaint myself with this world of light, even as the stars above disappear in the wake of the halogen. Canada's Dark Sky Preserves are a welcome reminder that we all need to look up more.

START HERE: canadianbucketlist.com/darksky

ZIP THROUGH TIME IN THE CYPRESS HILLS

Straddling the border between two provinces, Cypress Hills Interprovincial Park contains the highest elevation to be found between the Rockies and Labrador. Not mountains, mind you (we're in the prairies, after all), but healthy hills that invite downhill mountain bikers as well as hikers, paddlers, and campers. Open year round, the park is a designated Dark Sky Preserve, contains twisted lodgepole pine forests, rare wild orchids, and includes a former whiskey trading post that is now the Fort Walsh National Historic Site.

When it comes to ziplining, I've found the experience is only as special as the environment in which you do it. This makes flying with Cypress Hills Eco Adventures particularly interesting. Operating May through September, their twenty-five-metre long sky bridge and six zips let you fly ten metres above the forest floor, through and over the forest. With a treetop adventure park, treetop drop, and climbing wall, this award-winning company believes in pushing your boundaries, just like any self-respecting bucket list. While you're in the area, you can stroll through the beautiful acreage of the Cypress Hills Vineyard and Winery, and also pop over to the town of Eastend to visit a local character, somewhat long in the sharp tooth. The country's most complete skeleton of a Tyrannosaurus rex, nicknamed "Scotty," was discovered by a local high school teacher in 1991, and is now on display in the town's excellent T.rex Discovery Centre.

START HERE: canadianbucketlisti.com/cypresshills

EXPLORE NORTH AMERICA'S LARGEST SAND DUNES

Twenty thousand years ago, 97 percent of Canada was covered by a thick sheet of ice. As the glaciers retreated, they left behind spectacular natural phenomena, including the Bay of Fundy, Newfoundland's Gros Morne, and an area in northern Saskatchewan that looks very much as if the Sahara has relocated to the boreal forests of Canada. The Athabasca Sand Dunes extend one hundred kilometres along the southern edge of Lake Athabasca. They are the result of glaciers depositing bedrock into a delta, receding and exposing the remains to thousands of years of erosive wind. Local Dené nations, on the other hand, believe the dunes were created by a giant beaver, which does seem more patriotic. Winds continue to expand

SASKATCHEWAN ↑

35

Where to Find Canadian Scorpions

Athabasca's dunes may look like a desert, but for the real thing
you have to head to the warmth of the west.

Forests, prairies, mountains, lakes: in Canada, a tiny desert has
to fight for respect. Osoyoos, B.C., is the only recognized semi-
arid desert in Canada. It has the country's lowest rainfall, highest
recorded temperatures, and warmest lake. Located in the South
Okanagan, this desert zone is home to a hundred rare plants and
three hundred rare invertebrates, and it shelters the country's
only tarantulas and scorpions. Being Canadian, these fearsome
critters tend to apologize for causing any inconvenience. ➤

the dunes, by as much as 1.5 metres a year, earning Athabasca the
title of the largest active sand surface in Canada — a sandpit the
entire country could play in.

This is not a desert. The dunes look over a huge freshwater lake,
which is fed by streams, steady rains, and winter snowmelt. The
water table can become high enough to foster productive nurseries
for grasses, trees, and shrubs, attracting birds, animals, and insects.
Standing at the top of a thirty-metre-high dune, gazing south, certainly plays tricks on the mind, like finding an outdoor ice hockey
rink in central Saudi Arabia. Canada does have true deserts: the
semi-arid Osoyoos and the soft sand in the Yukon's Carcross, recognized by Guinness as the World's Smallest Desert. Yet the size of
Athabasca makes it *look* like a desert and not a freak of nature.

Athabasca Sand Dunes Provincial Wilderness Park is protected
by legislation, although its way-out-there location is just as effective.
The province's most remote park is only accessible via float plane
and boat, and according to the official website, it contains "no communities, permanent residents, services, facilities or roads of any kind."
That last bit is important, in case you expect communities of Ewoks,

sky-roads, and underground toilets. That being said, the Fond du Lac First Nation have a reserve adjacent to the park, and they use the dunes to hunt, trap, and collect medicinal plants, as they always have.

The area is ecologically unusual and extremely fragile, containing three hundred plant species, including ten endangered plants you simply won't find anywhere else in the world. Hard-core wilderness lovers can fly in and camp in six designated camping areas, packing everything in and out so as not to disturb the natural environment in any way. Float planes deposit visitors at Canterra Lake, or you can boat into Thompson Bay. It's a day hike to the sand giants that make up the William River dune fields, through subarctic forest and plants adapted to this unique environment. Since no camping is allowed among the dunes themselves, you must return to your campsite, where you can be alone in absolute wilderness, give or take a billion bugs or two. As someone who's hiked in dunes before, I can assure you the fun wears off just as quickly as your shoes fill with sand. Still, there's something to be said for climbing a tall, kilometre-long sand dune, and something even more wonderful about doing such a thing in Canada.

START HERE: canadianbucketlist.com/dunes

HORSE RIDE WITH BISON

Highway 12 slices through the wheat fields north of Saskatoon, a never-ending runway as flat as a boardroom table. Our destination is Prince Albert National Park, less than three hours as the crow flies or, more accurately, plucks road kill from the highway. The speed limit on these roads is one hundred kilometres per hour, a perversely slow clip for a mid-size rental sedan, or any horseless carriage for that matter. It's memories of galloping horses keeping me awake at the wheel: the time I raced across the green plains of Mongolia; that day I cantered on a Bedouin's horse in the Jordanian desert; exploring *Lord of the Rings* locations on horseback in New Zealand; learning to ride a unicorn Lipizzaner in the training rings of Slovenia. The Great Prairies Bucket List is kicking for an equine adventure, and Sturgeon River Ranch is ready to put us back in the saddle.

We turn off Highway 55, driving twenty-six kilometres on a dirt road through the West Gate entrance of the 3,874-square-kilometre

A Brush with Extinction

For a beast so large, it's frightening to think that North American bison almost went the way of the passenger pigeon, once among the most abundant birds on Earth, hunted to extinction in the late 1800s. It is estimated that 20 to 30 million bison once roamed the plains of America, but after decades of unchecked and wholesale slaughter, largely by fur traders, bison numbers had decreased to just over 1,000 by the late 1800s. Today, there are around 500,000 bison in North America, of which only 15,000 can be found roaming in their natural range. ➤

national park. Across the river are three generations of Vaadelands, a family that settled here in 1928, the same year the park was founded. Operating cattle, land, and horses, Gord Vaadeland took a different route when he founded Sturgeon River Ranch as a horse riding and adventure operator, successfully integrating both his business and his family's farms with Prince Albert's star attraction: Canada's only herd of free-ranging plains bison, roaming within their historic range. Gord is waiting for us, with his trademark wide-brimmed black cowboy hat and red checkered shirt. Two bold black horses will pull our supply wagon. Along for the ride, Gord's trusty sidekicks, Glen (hangdog moustache, slow prairie drawl) and Beckie (chef, bison naturalist, trail mom), and my dad, eager to believe that riding horses is like riding bicycles. It's been thirty years since he hopped in a saddle, and we're both hoping he can stay on it.

My horse is a tall brown speckled stallion named Applejack. He's got the race champion War Admiral twice in his lineage, but Gord assures me this apple has fallen miles from the tree. After years of commercial riders, Applejack is addicted to grazing on the same abundant sweetgrass attracting the bison. Still, the stallion is

certainly a step up from my usual brand of trail horse, with names like Haystack or Lego, as in "always falling apart."

Saddled up, we head into a dense forest of trembling aspen and wild hazelnut bush. Gord calls this the "Mantracker Trail." When the hit TV series filmed a couple of episodes in the area, Gord was the on-camera guide, while his horses tracked down the "prey." No crazy chases are expected for our overnight trip, but still, we're on a hunt: somewhere in the meadow clearings ahead are herds of wild bison, and our horses will help us find them. Wildlife viewing on horseback is ideal, explains Gord. The park's animals don't get spooked, and our horses will detect any wildlife long before we do.

As we plod along in single file, the landscape quickly proves there's so much more to the prairie than flat farmland. Jackson, Gord's feisty horse, perks up his ears. Up ahead is a black bear, oblivious to our approach. With the wind in our favour, we ride closer and closer, until the bear suddenly realizes we're just feet away and quickly darts into the forest. Next is a lone bison bull, a tank of a beast, grazing in a meadow. We approach quietly and carefully. Having grown up in these woods, Gord knows never to corner a bison and the value of keeping your distance. "They can probably outrun your horse," he whispers. Especially Applejack, who would probably stop for a snack in the middle of a stampede.

Two hundred years ago, there were millions of bison in North America, migrating across the plains. Their meat and fur supported First Nations tribes for millennia. But when European fur traders arrived, they hunted the bison to the verge of extinction. In 2008, there were 450 bison roaming Prince Albert. By 2014, that number had been reduced to just 240, the result of illegal poaching, increased wolf predation, and disease. While farmed bison are plentiful (their meat is a healthy alternative to beef), the genetic future of these wild bison is constantly under threat.

Riding through aspen and Jack pine forest that at times seems almost impenetrable, we arrive a few hours later at our tipis and campsite. As a licensed operator and wildlife consultant, Gord has special permission for his guests to spend the night here. Wagon unloaded, cots set up in the tipis, we sit around the fire, baking bannock on sticks in the fire to accompany Beckie's delicious wild elk stew. Gord pulls out a bottle of bourbon (a buffalo is on the label), the five of us enjoying a night of true prairie wilderness. As the fire crackles, the horses tense.

"Over here, quick!" says Glen.

Just across the river, a hundred feet away, a herd of thirty bison have wandered into a clearing to graze in the twilight. It's one of those magical, unexpected wildlife moments, when everything comes together: the people, the landscape, the weather, the animals. When it gets too dark, we sit around the fire, listening to the herd make its way upriver. Retiring to the rustic comforts of the tipi, we hear the patter of raindrops on the soft walls, the howl of a wolf in the distance.

Thinking of the area's glittering lakes, fun characters, wild animals, and even wilder summer celebrations at Ness Creek, I fall sound asleep in little doubt that the plains of central Saskatchewan have much to offer the Prairies Bucket List.

START HERE: canadianbucketlist.com/princealbert

A TALE OF TWO HOTELS

There are many worthy hotels, inns, B&Bs, and resorts in the Prairies. Our bucket list, however, favours the extraordinary, like the river view to be had from the sixth floor of Saskatoon's imposing Bessborough. During my stay, I gazed out the window at castle turrets and the arches of University Bridge crossing the South Saskatchewan River. Then I pinched myself, just to make sure I hadn't slipped through a wormhole and popped up somewhere in Paris. But before I ring room service for a bottle of champagne and some *petit bonbons*, we must close our eyes and teleport to Regina's Hotel Saskatchewan.

It is the early twentieth century, and the Canadian Pacific Railway is enjoying much success with their opulent and grand European château–style hotels in Quebec, Ontario, and the Rockies. Built to encourage wealthy travellers to use their railways (first), spend money (second), and discover the wonders of travel (third), the CPR has decided that the Queen City is ready for its own hotel. CPR's competitor, the Grand Trunk Pacific Railway, did try this first, and planned to build the Château Qu'Appelle, a turreted Scottish baronial masterpiece, on the corner of Albert Street and College Avenue. Alas, construction was halted when the railway declared bankruptcy. A decade later, the old steel beams of the Qu'Appelle were

Canada's Grand Railway Hotels

- The Empress Hotel (Victoria)
- The Hotel Vancouver
- The Banff Springs
- The Château Lake Louise
- Jasper Park Lodge
- The Palliser Hotel (Calgary)
- The Hotel Macdonald (Edmonton)
- The Bessborough (Saskatoon)
- The Hotel Saskatchewan (Regina)
- The Fort Garry Hotel (Winnipeg)
- The Royal York (Toronto)
- Château Laurier (Ottawa)
- Château Frontenac (Quebec City)
- Château Montebello (Montebello, Quebec)
- The Algonquin Resort (St. Andrews-by-the-Sea, NB)
- The Nova Scotian (Halifax) ➤

heading to Victoria Street to be used in the construction of the lavish Hotel Saskatchewan. Although it would follow the style of the luxurious interiors of other Canadian grand railway hotels, the addition of turrets and gargoyles to the facade would make way for a towering, less ostentatious landmark.

Opened in 1927, the ten-storey, 224-room Hotel Saskatchewan has hosted everyone from British royalty to the Rolling Stones (who famously booked out most of the hotel for a series of concerts in 2006). I've had the good fortune to stay at the hotel on several occasions, and besides the wonderfully central location, friendly staff, and the hotel's sense of occasion, I always enjoy experiencing part of Saskatchewan's history.

Back in 1927, Saskatoon's Board of Trade watched anxiously as Regina bathed in the glow of its CPR hotel. Saskatoon wanted in. The city petitioned CPR competitors Canadian National Railways (CNR), and the green light was given to build an imposing 225-room hotel on the riverfront. Modelled on a Bavarian castle, the project was an opportunity for the CNR to one-up the CPR, constructing the kind of palatial hotel that Walt Disney would be proud of. It would be named after the brazen, pompously-named governor general of the day, Sir Vere Brabazon Ponsonby, the Ninth Earl of Bessborough. Ironically, when the CNR hit financial difficulties, the Canadian Pacific Railway had to come in for some last-minute financial CPR. The Bessborough

Hotel opened for business in 1935, and today, Saskatonians refer to it affectionately as "The Bez." A highlight of the city's skyline, the Bess has undergone several major renovations, and the "Castle on the River" continues to contribute to Saskatoon's reputation as the "Paris of the Prairies."

TRACK WOLVES IN THE SNOW

The prairies meet the boreal forests in Prince Albert National Park, which is bordered by dense forests of birch, aspen, and spruce, creating beautiful panoramas in an area that hosts one of the most elusive creatures in Canada's wildlife pantheon — the grey wolf.

The largest of the wild dog species, the grey wolf can travel up to seventy kilometres a day when hunting. They tend to live in packs of between five and twelve individuals, ruled by an alpha pair, a male and female that generally mate for life. Prey like deer, elk, and hare are often bigger or faster, which is why wolves employ co-operative hunting strategies, and even surprise ambushes. Not that you're likely to see a kill, or even a wolf, for that matter. It's always a gamble when it comes to wildlife in Canada, which one might say has too much space for too few animals. Still, Prince Albert National

Park is one of the world's best places to encounter wolves, especially during the winter. Much of the park is deserted during the freeze, but their prey is abundant.

Guided sled dog or vehicle excursions will often discover hand-size wolf prints, scat droppings, or yellow patches of urine in the snow where the animals have marked their territory. The fortunate among us might see wolves along a road, or chasing prey across a frozen lake. I would argue that anyone who gets the opportunity to join Brad Muir's wonderful Sundogs Excursions for an overnight sledding adventure is fortunate, regardless. Alternatively, visit the Park in summer to join the wolf howl — when park interpreters lead a caravan of cars to the forest's edge for a man–beast conversation. The distinctive wolf howl, heard in any season, is not just the call of the Canadian wild, it's the roar of our Great Prairies Bucket List.

START HERE: canadianbucketlist.com/princealbertnationalpark

MEET THE FIRST NATIONS

Tyrone Tootoosis, the imposing curator and manager of cultural resources at the Wanuskewin Heritage Park, squints his eyes, looking out over the valley corridor. "When I grew up, we didn't have air conditioning ... just a cold wife," he says.

"But I guess that made her a hot wife in winter," I reply.

"Yes, Robin, and you know, back then, Running Water was just somebody's name."

I'm laughing at the joke, but I'm laughing with gratitude, too. Tyrone's humour has put me at ease as I wrap my head around the First Nations of Canada. Aboriginals? Natives? Indians? I've seen their legacy across the country, but I've come to Wanuskewin, a short drive from Saskatoon, to finally understand who these Canadians are, what they believe in, and why the scars run so deep.

Aboriginal Tourist Destinations

Learn more about Canada's First Nations at these excellent destinations:

1. Wanuskewin Heritage Park, Saskatoon, SK
2. Canadian Aboriginal Festival, Toronto, ON
3. Haida Heritage Centre, Skidegate, BC
4. Blackfoot Crossing Historical Park, Siksika First Nation, AB
5. Stampede Indian Village, Calgary, AB
6. Fort William Historical Park, Thunder Bay, ON
7. Squamish Lil'wat Cultural Centre, Whistler, BC
8. Champagne & Aishihik Da Ku Cultural Centre, Haines Junction, YK
9. Unikkaarvik Visitors Centre, Iqaluit, NU
10. Musée de Saint-Boniface, Saint-Boniface, MB ➤

Tyrone's long black hair is braided and parted in the fashion of the Plains Cree. He's got the look of a noble actor (he's appeared on screen), earrings, beads shaking from a waistcoat. Over a delicious pulled bison sandwich at the park's restaurant, Tyrone immediately puts things in perspective. "When people say, 'Tell us about the First Nations,' it's like arriving in Europe and saying, 'Tell us about the white man.'"

There are some 700,000 Native Canadians belonging to more than 630 bands spread out across the country — bands with different languages, cultures, and customs. One of the challenges for the Wanuskewin Heritage Park, a National Historic Site located on land with six thousand years of Aboriginal history, is to help visitors understand this. Another is to create a community where old wounds can heal, for all people of the Northern Plains, and forgotten traditions can once again thrive. "We have the responsibility to tell our own story, and not necessarily through history. Aboriginal tourism is not just something to tick off, it's about discovering a comfort zone," says Tyrone. A comfort zone I didn't know existed.

We take a walk along one of the paths in the 240-hectare grounds. Tyrone explains what a powwow is: three days and three nights of dancing and singing. "If people want Indian culture, they should visit Bombay. We're the First Nations," he says proudly. Nations that

communicate in a language of nature and spirits, where everything is connected to everything else. Nations that believe they have always lived on these lands — before the ice age, before Europeans arrived, before the residential schools that were cruelly implemented to annihilate their culture. Tyrone's grandfather was a "radical" and raised his family away from the Canadian government's shocking attempt to rip apart the fabric of First Nations culture. Tyrone never went to the schools, and he grew up proud.

We look at the remains of a medicine wheel as old as Stonehenge. So much oral history has been lost, nobody is quite sure what it was designed for. Back in the park's galleries, which host schools, training sessions, festivals, and events, we watch a young man (and two young boys) perform a mind-boggling hoop dance. A special exhibition honours the horse, known as Mistatim, literally "big dog." Tyrone explains to me the importance of elders, the custodians of the community, and leads me to an elder named Norm McQuill. I've been encouraged to ask the difficult questions. "Why are the First Nations seemingly so down and out? How come there's so little integration? Where does all the government money go?" It's a lively discussion, and Norm's answers surprise me.

With so much pain in the past, Norm believes the First Nations must take responsibility for their own futures. He rues the corruption of tribal councils, the breakdown of First Nations values. Tyrone brings over a young man who had overheard us in the gallery. "Sorry to interrupt, but this is important," he says.

The young man presents two cigarettes to his elder, according to the tobacco tradition, and begins to tell his story. He was sent away to a residential school, lost all touch with his family and culture, and is visiting from Alberta to begin the long journey home. He asks Norm if he knows of some of his relatives, and it turns out that Norm does indeed. In fact, Norm is a relative, too. The young man trembles, his eyes riding waves of tears, the swells of happiness and disaster. It's an honour to witness a moment nobody has prepared for. An honour to be allowed a glimpse into a vibrant and rich world that has so much to offer, even for just one afternoon. One doesn't have to visit Wanuskewin to embrace First Nations culture in Canada. Yet the heritage park's exhibits, history, land, and personalities make it a great place to start.

START HERE: canadianbucketlist.com/wanuskewin

SASKATCHEWAN

PRAIRIE PADDLES

How's this for a bucket list canoe adventure? Traversing a famed Voyageur route along the Churchill River. The river itself flows over the Precambrian Shield, into a series of lakes linked by rapids and falls, and crosses forests and rocky outcroppings. Enjoyed by both seasoned pros and beginners, this particular trip takes you 105 kilometres from Sandfly Lake to Otter Rapids, navigating nine portages up to three hundred metres in length. Churchill River

Canoe Outfitters arrange for equipment, transportation, and cabins on either end of the journey. And there'll be plenty of time to view wildlife, see ancient rock paintings, and feast on shore lunches and campfire BBQs. Tours operate from May to September. The bugs are typically worse in June than they are in August, and the fishing in August is outstanding. As for the water, it's so clean that some paddlers drink it right out of the river.

START HERE: canadianbucketlist.com/churchillriver

CUT THE MUSTARD

Here's something you probably didn't know: 70 percent of Canada's mustard seed is produced in Saskatchewan. Now consider that Canada is the world's largest producer of pure mustard seed, accounting for approximately one third of the world crop, with over half the market share of world exports. You know that bottle of Dijon you picked up in France last year? Before the piquant seeds were ground into paste, they grew here, under the hot prairie sun.

The Romans are credited with inventing the sauce, skimming the must off unfermented grapes (also used in Balsamic vinegar), and adding the seeds for spiciness. "Burning must" in Latin: *mustem ardens*, hence, mustard. And that nuclear-yellow gloop that Americans slather all over their hot dogs at Yankee Stadium? Blame Canada. Along with lentils and chickpeas, Saskatchewan produces the vast majority of this mouth-watering seed. Beyond growing it, the province also studies it, prepares it, cooks with it, and relishes it each year at Regina's Great Saskatchewan Mustard Festival. Likewise, *The Great Canadian Prairies Bucket List* relishes the opportunity to celebrate a condiment that, despite its mustard hues, is distinctly red and white.

Oh, mighty mustard! Tomato sauce is sugary and mayonnaise milky, but mustard sends a quiver down the culinary spine. What is a roast beef sandwich without mustard? A hot dog? A ham? Mustard seeds have been an integral spice in global cuisines for millennia, from the curries of Asia to the condiments of Europe. Buddha used it to illustrate the universality of suffering. Jesus compared the Kingdom of God to a mustard seed, from whence the mite of a seed can grow tall and proud. There are three distinct types of seed:

Know Your Mustard

It's easy enough to create your own table mustard. Get some mustard flour, add water or vinegar, and voila! American yellow mustard uses yellow seeds, the largest of the species with the highest oil content. Deli sandwiches love the sharpness of brown mustard. Dijon is typically made with white wine, and despite the grumblings, is not exclusive to the region in France. You can mix fruits, peppers, and other vegetables with mustard to create relishes, and add spirits and beers. Because of its natural antibacterial qualities, mustard does not have to be refrigerated, although it will lose colour and flavour over time. ➤

brown, oriental, and the most popular, yellow (usually brightened with the addition of turmeric).

Our journey begins at Ackerman Acres outside of Moose Jaw. Here we meet a cheerful mustard-grower by the name of Patrick Ackerman on his six thousand acres. Sweeping up a handful of seeds and popping them in my mouth, the seed delivers an instant wasabi rush to the head. Patrick explains how seeds are dispersed and harvested with enormous machines and combines. Cleansed and sold to international markets by the pound, it's a hardy crop suited for cold climates and wet soils. I ask Patrick why the French don't grow their own seeds.

SASKATCHEWAN ↑

"Oh, they tried," he explains, "but they couldn't get the quality of our seeds, our taste, our oiliness." Mustard is grown in countries like Russia, China, and the United States, but Canadian seeds are prized above all. Perhaps the secret ingredient lies within the Prairies.

Chef Jssel Blackmore at Sprouts Catering in Regina has a few secret ingredients of her own. Trained in Vancouver, she returned to her hometown to start the catering business with her sister Hayley. Jssel has won the coveted Mustard Jersey (think the Tour de France for mustard freaks) at the Great Saskatchewan Mustard Festival, where chefs compete with recipes and homemade sauces. There's a gleam of pride in her eye when I sample her homemade Apple Butter Mustard, Cranberry Mustard, and biting Hot Mustard. It's a world apart from the nuclear banana–coloured paste that's squeezed onto a hot dog. Jssel roasts her own seeds, combines them with vinegar and spices, and bottles them herself. Unlike the popular Gravelbourg mustards produced in Saskatchewan, these are sold only in her store. For now.

Chef Malcolm at Beer Bros is the *enfant terrible* in Regina's local mustard scene. Known for his creative recipes, he's invited me over to taste some of his mustard-infused dishes — paired with craft beers, of course. Originally from Southampton, England, Malcolm arrived in the Prairies with his future Canadian wife a dozen years ago. "It was December. When I got off the plane, I basically froze to the tarmac." He laughs. "Well, she warned me it would be cold."

He explains how mustard seed is used to tenderize and flavour meats, how oriental seeds produce spicier mustards, as the name might suggest. Then he orders a round of deep-fried, panko-crusted avocado to dip in Gravelbourg's cranberry mustard. It's a combination of flavours and textures that tattoos itself in my culinary memory. Hot baked pretzels follow for dipping in Malcolm's homemade mustard pilsner sauce, and are capped off with a juicy mustard-coffee rubbed trout. We chase it all down with Sriracha beer from Oregon's Rogue Brewery, because chili is feeling left out. In Saskatoon's Ayden Kitchen and Bar, the mixologist experiments with a mustard cocktail. Although he's a little nervous about the results, he nails it. Saskatchewan's success with mustard, however, is no accident.

"Please, no video cameras," asks Dr. Bifang Cheng when I visit the Agriculture and Agri-food Canada Research Centre in Saskatoon. I don't know if this is because she's shy, or doesn't want me to accidentally reveal any trade secrets. This is the largest facility of its kind dedicated to mustard seeds, and nobody knows more about the genetics and science of the herb than Dr. Cheng. For Canada to keep its export quality up, the researchers need to ensure the seeds maintain and hopefully improve their oil content, proteins, and taste. Cross pollination creates pods and seeds that are hardier, more resistant to bugs, more plentiful in the field. I feel like I've stepped into a biology textbook, the kind I largely used as pillows during my high school classes. While I understand little of the science, there's no doubt that very smart, dedicated people are on the job, ensuring that Canadian mustard continues to dominate.

Prefer mayonnaise? Without mustard seed, your mayonnaise is as bland as damp cotton wool. Without mustard seed, you can kiss your coleslaw goodbye and remove the tickle from your pickles. Along with growers, chefs, scientists, and foodies, the Great Saskatchewan Mustard Festival sows the seeds for mustard appreciation on the Prairies Bucket List. Make some space, maple syrup. It's time we give Canada's contribution to global cooking its turn in the mustard-yellow spotlight.

START HERE: canadianbucketlist.com/mustard

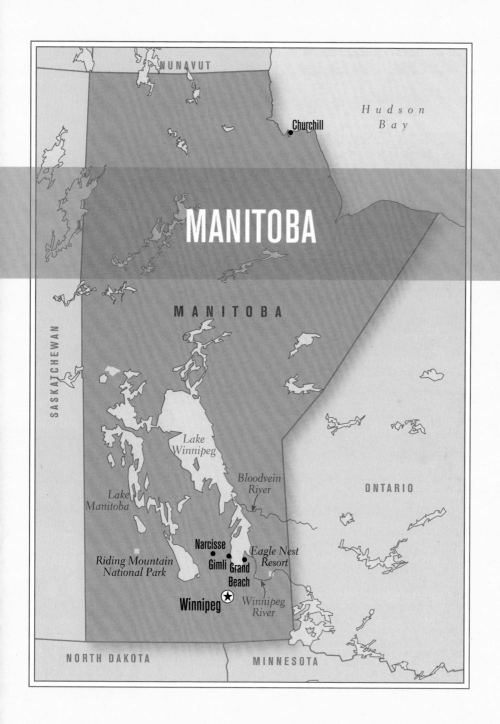

SEE POLAR BEARS FROM A TUNDRA BUGGY

Standing on the outdoor viewing platform of one of Frontier North's customized Tundra Buggies, I gaze at the permafrost of northern Manitoba. Two polar bears are on their hind legs, sparring like boxers, oblivious to the fact they are providing one of the most spectacular animal encounters you can experience anywhere. I'm wearing two thermal under-layers and a layer of fleece beneath my parka, but what does it matter if my nose is an icicle? Watching the largest carnivore on Earth in its natural habitat lights a fire under your soul.

Each October and November, hungry bears along the southwest coast of Hudson Bay emerge

Is that a Pizzly or a Grolar Bear?

Melting polar ice caps are sending polar bears farther south, just as human development is pushing grizzly bears farther north. While the two species would have encountered each other in the past, there's evidence that for the first time these two different species are mating to produce hybrids: white bears with larger heads, grizzly humps and brown streaks, and brown bears with white patches, known to feast on seals. DNA testing on a pizzly shot by a hunter confirmed it was indeed a hybrid. A half-dozen wild pizzlys (also known as grolars, prizzlys, or nanulak) have been spotted on Victoria Island, and as the Arctic continues to melt, scientists anticipate the numbers will grow. Since pizzly bears are not considered polar bears, they are not protected from hunters. ➤

from a state scientists call walking hibernation, in which they reduce their metabolisms while waiting for the ice to freeze. When it does, they'll head north and break their long summer fast. Cool ocean currents in the bay freeze these waters early, making the small bay-side community of Churchill the most southerly point for humans to encounter polar bears. The nine-hundred-plus bears that annually migrate through this region are joined by thousands of tourists, scientists, media, and students, all excited by this unique wildlife encounter. It is not uncommon for bears to wander directly into town. Surrounded by bear traps, Churchill is closely monitored on camera, and famously has a jail for offending bears that continue to pose a problem. We're advised to stick within certain town limits, with polar bear warning signs reinforcing the message. Considering that Churchill's population shares the landscape with hundreds of hungry bears, it is remarkable there haven't been any human fatalities for decades. In fact, Churchill has become an example of how humans and wildlife can safely live together.

We're not ten minutes from the airport, seated in a school bus shuttle, when we spot our first bear. Fellow passengers around me explode into action: cameras, whoops, sighs, even tears. A solitary sub-adult male bear is ambling over rocks close to the bay. He stands on his hind legs like a giant meerkat, observing us with curious eyes. Although the bear has yet to feed after a long summer, there's no doubting he is a magnificent creature: shag-carpet hair the colour of

MANITOBA ↑

65

a vanilla milkshake, round furry ears, a black button nose. Polar bears look too cuddly to be hungry carnivores, but a loaded rifle above our driver's seat reminds us otherwise. These bears can run up to forty kilometres an hour, and with one of the best noses in the animal kingdom, can smell prey from miles away. Camouflaged against the snow, these ruthless hunters are perfectly adapted to be at the top of the Arctic food chain, with no natural enemies — save humans, and the rapid disappearance of their habitat.

Elated from our first sighting, we transfer to a Tundra Buggy for the ninety-minute drive to Frontier North's Tundra Buggy Lodge. The forty-passenger buggy sits on 1.7-metre tires above a customized fire truck chassis. Heated by a propane furnace, it has anti-fog windows, an eagle-eyed driver, and a handy latrine at the back (it's way too dangerous to step outside, and besides, good luck finding a tree on the tundra). The "road" is a rough, bouncy mud track, but all discomfort vanishes when we spot several more bears, anxiously waiting for the ice to

freeze. Hundreds of photographs are taken as we observe them for a half-hour. Docking to the impressive hundred-metre-long lodge on wheels, we settle into the bunks, kitchen, and lounge for the next few days. Since the lodge is located at a particular gathering point for bears, the onboard crew don't touch ground for the entire eight-week season. The price of the excursion is steep, but nobody is complaining about sharing quarters. We're here for one reason — polar bears — and fortunately, nobody is going home disappointed.

For the next three days, we spend eight hours a day roaming the tundra and are treated to a polar bear extravaganza. Multiple male pairs

spar just metres from our windows, exerting their dominance for the winter to come. Large, curious bears stand up on their hind legs against our buggy, their warm breath literally fogging up our camera lenses. A lone bear walks across a frozen lake, backlit by the low afternoon sun. It's a photographer's dream, and pure heaven for a polar bear enthusiast. Arctic foxes, hares, and gyrfalcons also make an appearance, as do boxes of wine, great food, interesting presentations, and wonderful company.

The bears around Churchill are among the most threatened of the estimated twenty thousand polar bears remaining in the Arctic. They're also the most accessible. Frontier North's Tundra Buggy adventure is without a doubt something to experience before you die. Although, sadly, with melting sea ice, rising sea levels, and the increasing threat to their natural habitat, you might want to act before the polar bears surrounding Churchill beat you to it.

START HERE: canadianbucketlist.com/polarbear

SNORKEL WITH BELUGAS

Y ou can thank *two* large white animals for putting Churchill on the
map: the most southerly population of polar bears in the winter,
and, in summer, the thousands of beluga whales that gather where
the Churchill River pours into Hudson Bay. Snorkelling typically
involves bright coral, tropical fish, and at least one kid surrounded
by a suspicious yellow haze. Well, we're in Canada, and in Canada,
our experiences are big, bold, and bucket list–worthy. That's why,
when the weather is favourable, we'll don thick wetsuits, head into
Hudson Bay on a Zodiac, and search for a particularly inviting pod
of belugas. Fins, heads, humps, and tails are everywhere, and with
their doe eyes and flexible necks, belugas seem particularly friendly
and curious. Hopping into the frigid five-degrees-Celsius water is

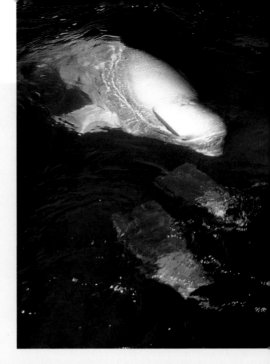

something of a shock to the system, but since hundreds of whales are in your general vicinity, think of the initial splash as a defibrillator for the soul. Holding on to a rope attached to the raft, the shade of the water is less Caribbean-blue and more Arctic-murk. With your affable guide on the lookout, the belugas swim around you, gazing with their prominent melon-heads, singing with distinctive canary-like calls, diving deep or breaching above. Given the abundance of whales, the responsible practices of the tour operators, and the relative scarcity of snorkellers each summer, whale biologists do not believe the animals are negatively impacted by the human presence. With the limited visibility, you won't really know where to look, or where the next grinning whale might suddenly appear. Depending on the beluga activity (and your ability to withstand the extreme cold), your underwater excursion might last mere minutes or up to an hour. Sure, we won't find Nemo snorkelling in Hudson Bay, but our bucket list far prefers this once-in-a-lifetime encounter with a one-of-a-kind animal anyway.

START HERE: canadianbucketlist.com/beluga

CRACK THE HERMETIC CODE

Things you may not know about Winnipeg:

- It was the first city in the world to introduce the 911 emergency response system.
- It's residents consume the most Slurpees in the world.
- Winnipeggers inspired James Bond and invented the cellphone.
- It hosted the biggest gold heist in Canadian history.
- The Manitoba Legislature is actually a mysterious temple with codes and clues that have been deciphered to reveal six thousand years of architectural magic.

A local academic named Frank Albo expects you to scratch your head at that last one. He'll also appreciate the symbolism in my choice of five, not four or six, factoids about Winnipeg. A long-time

student of the esoteric, Frank initially noticed some architectural weirdness on the sphinxes guarding the Manitoba Legislature. He decided to investigate, and ten years later he cracked a century-old code built into the imposing government building that reveals far more than anyone could possibly have imagined. Frank has since become an expert on Freemasonry, architectural symbolism, and the occult. While his bestselling book *The Hermetic Code* opens the doors of perception, his evening tours personally invite you to join him at the Legislature, swallow the blue pill, and follow him down the rabbit hole. Since he introduced the Hermetic Code Tour in 2009, more than ten thousand people have done exactly that, and today, joining two dozen tourists, I will be one of them.

A handsome, slim, dark-haired Albo arrives fashionably late, wearing torn jeans and well-worn boots. Given his academic prowess,

Canada's Great Mysteries

The fascinating mystery of the Manitoba Legislature has been solved, but the jury is still out on these classic Canadian mysteries.

1. **The *Mary Celeste*:** Built in Nova Scotia, a stocked, seaworthy vessel is mysteriously abandoned in the middle of the Atlantic, leaving everything intact, including the captain's logbook.
2. **Tom Thomson:** Group of Seven artist mysteriously found dead in Algonquin Park's Canoe Lake, a fishing line wrapped around his leg and plenty of speculation about love, cash, and war motives.
3. **Where Is Vinland?** L'Anse aux Meadows proved that Europeans visited North America earlier than anyone had thought, but Viking sagas speak of a land rich in grapes called Vinland, which remains to be found.
4. **Shag Harbour UFOs:** In 1967, several locals (including an RCMP constable) watched four bright lights flash in the sky, dive toward the sea, hover over the water, and slowly disappear, leaving an odd yellow foam in their wake. Was it a UFO, or a secret military weapon?
5. **Canadian creatures:** How do we explain dozens of sightings of Okanagan Lake's Ogopogo lake monster, the Sasquatch, or the popularity of Justin Bieber? ➤

everyone was expecting a bookworm. Frank's enthusiasm for the subject, and his skill in bringing life to the stone, is immediately apparent. "I assure you, you will never look at architecture the same way," he tells us. "On the surface it's a house of government, but this building is a Sudoku puzzle in stone, built by grand masters and keepers of ancient secrets."

These are heady words, and Frank challenges everyone to question, to not believe. He knows how flighty these claims sound if not supported by physical evidence. It is the physical evidence, as solid as the Legislature's imposing concrete pillars, that makes this ninety-minute tour unmissable.

FACT: Every person involved in the construction of this building was a Freemason, as were nearly a century's worth of consecutive Manitoba premiers.

FACT: The Freemasons were traditionally custodians of the design of the original Temple of God, passed down through the ages under great secrecy.

FACT: The architect Frank W. Simon was a master Freemason, a professor of architecture, a man who placed nothing by ornament and designed everything with utmost thought given to the hermetic principles of numerology, astrology, geometry, and alchemy.

Frank walks us outside and points to the statues overlooking the entrance. They are infused with special significance, representing two deities, Manitoba and Winnipeg, based on ancient gods, Hermes and Aphrodite. Even the pillars are measured to temple specifications. And as for the famous Golden Boy on the top? Surrounded by the four elements, it's Hermes himself, placed as the alchemic fifth essence, the quintessential symbol of enlightenment, and the hero of the architectural craft. It's heady stuff, but Frank's obvious passion, clear voice, and sense of humour keep everyone fully engaged.

Inside the entrance, he points out more ancient temple similarities: guarding bison, protective amulets energized with sunlight, and the repetition of the significant numbers 13, 8, and 5: there are 13 lights on every floor, 13 stones in the archway, 3 sets of 13 steps, and 8 pointed stars. The details would require a book (hence Frank's bestseller), but symbol after symbol, fact after fact, prove that Simon's building is a Rosetta Stone of mystical architecture, challenging Winnipeggers to decipher its accurate recreation of the Biblical temple, chiselled in concrete, hidden in plain view. There is even a Holy of Holies, in this case the lieutenant governor's office, off limits to outsiders, protecting a symbolic Ark of the Covenant behind purple curtains. Like the original Holy of Holies, it is accessed on just one day of the year.

Frank peppers his tour with entertaining anecdotes, such as how he convinced the premier to support his research, how members of the Assembly thought he was bonkers, and how he was accosted one night while doing research in his pajamas. When he discovered Simon's own writings about the creation of a symbolic altar over marble with veins specifically aligned to symbolize blood, even he got a little spooked.

After shattering the traditional understanding of the Legislature's large mural, we head downstairs and stand in a circle around the Pool of the Black Star. During the day, government officials cross this star with scant regard for its intense symbolism and architectural genius. "Architecture is frozen music. You can read dimensions like notes. With the large dome visible through the thirteen-foot altar above your head, at this spot you're speaking in fifths, literally speaking with the power of Hermes." His voice echoes and booms through the empty building. He invites us each to stand in the star and try for ourselves. It feels as if I've entered a sound bubble; my voice deepens, swells, and reverberates around me. Six thousand years of architectural mystery unfold, and my neck hairs stand up.

The great architect Frank W. Simon took his design secrets to the grave, and so the symbolism at the Legislature would have remained a complete mystery, an anomaly, another quirk in a quirky city. One man spent ten years figuring it out, and he's absolutely right: after standing in the Pool of the Black Star, you will never look at buildings the same way again.

START HERE: canadianbucketlist.com/hermetic

GET CREEPY AT THE NARCISSE SNAKE DENS

I used to be petrified of snakes, a condition many a reader will relate to. Even though we are much bigger than all but the biggest of serpents, and even though most of them are completely harmless (not to mention painfully shy), they nevertheless instill terror at the very thought of them. Slithering, fork-tongued, sharp-fanged, poisonous killers waiting in the shadows to strike! I'm convinced our fear of these reptiles has something to do with the Bible, where the snake was picked out early as representative of a far greater evil.

In any event, I've found a way to conquer the fears that hold us back. Afraid of heights? Go skydiving. Claustrophobic? Go caving. Afraid of sharks? Jump into a cage and swim with a great white. Afraid of snakes? Adopt one as a pet. Which is what I did, in my early twenties — a metre-long North American corn snake. To be honest, I never quite got over my fear of old Aquarius the Dog, as she was named, which might explain why she attacked me frequently. Corn

MANITOBA

Relax, This Isn't Australia

Red garter snakes are perfectly harmless. This isn't Australia, which has the Top 11 most venomous snakes in the world, and that doesn't include *Matrix* actor Hugo Weaving. Canada has twenty-four species of snake, the largest of which is Ontario's harmless black rat snake, which grows to over two metres. Vipers such as massasauga and western rattlesnakes can be nasty, but encounters are so rare you're in far more danger of getting stung by a bee. ➤

snakes are constrictors, and although she could wrap herself tightly around my arm, she could do no more harm to me than an infant with a plastic toy. She could, however, strike for no reason, quickly, with a cold-blooded stare, sensing my fear and pouncing on it. Aquarius went missing one day, and we found her three weeks later living in my bedroom hi-fi speaker, inches from my head. After that, we named her Sony. Snakes make great pets: they're super low maintenance, increase in value with age, and scare the bejesus out of any intruders. Strangers don't knock on doors with Beware of Snake signs.

All this to say I was delighted to learn that 130 kilometres from Winnipeg lies the largest congregation of any vertebrate species on Earth. Twice a year, a natural phenomenon takes place that blankets the wetland region of Interlake with tens of thousands of snakes. In spring, typically late April or early May, males literally crawl over themselves in an effort to impress one female. The result is a landscape writhing and bubbling with serpents — in the crevices of their limestone dens, in the trees, on the rocks. Managed by Manitoba Conservation, a three-kilometre-long interpretive trail has been established so visitors can watch all this from the comfort of the other side of the fence. Researchers believe there are up to 150,000 snakes living in these dens, located six kilometres from the town of Narcisse,

off Highway 17. To prevent the automotive slaughter of thousands of snakes, tunnels run under the roads to funnel garters away from harmful traffic. Visitors are allowed to pick up the snakes, so long as they are gentle and release them unharmed. Red garters are quite thin and don't grow much longer than your arm.

Under a pile of one hundred male snakes might be one female, noticeably larger than the boys on her back. Rubbing their chins all over the female, the males are courting amidst stiff competition, creating what scientists call a mating ball (a similar phenomenon might be observed on the dance floors of adolescent nightclubs). The female will select only one lucky male, and then, together with the rest of the snakes, disappear into the wetlands for the summer to gorge on frogs, insects, and other unlucky participants in the wetland food chain. Come autumn, the snakes return to their dens, in another brief period when you can watch this reptilian phenomenon. The snakes survive the freezing Manitoba winters by huddling up by the thousands in these limestone sinkholes, slowing their metabolisms down and turning their blood to the thickness of mayonnaise in a process known as brumation.

Come on, Esrock! Is this really something to see in Manitoba before I kick the bucket?

Look, let's not snake around the issue: this is as unique and squirmy as it gets. Plus, Canada is not Australia, cursed with many of the world's deadliest snakes. You can't pick up taipans or black tiger snakes, since they are not nearly as polite as a red garter snake. True Canadian snakes, then, involved in a truly unusual natural spectacle.

START HERE: canadianbucketlist.com/snakes

WATCH THE ROYAL WINNIPEG BALLET IN THE PARK

I view ballet the way my wife views rugby. We both see talent at work, years of dedication by the participants, poetry of motion, and the wonderful opportunity to ogle excellent specimens of the human leg. Neither of us is sure what the rules are, or the levels of difficulty, but we can sit through it, knowing we appreciate each other's company. Point being, I'm not the ideal candidate to convince you that watching the Royal Winnipeg Ballet dance their magic belongs on the Prairies Bucket List. And yet I must, because it does.

If in doubt, simply ask yourself: how is it that a city in the Canadian Prairies boasts one of the world's most respected, sought-after, and watched ballet companies? That's exactly what I asked Jeff Herd, the chief operating officer of the Royal Winnipeg Ballet.

MANITOBA

The Royal Canadian Bucket List?

There are dozens of Canadian institutions with a royal prefix, dating back to 1801, when King George III bestowed the honour on the Royal Institution for the Advancement of Learning, now known as McGill University. Queen Victoria gave us the Royal Canadian Golf Association and Royal Canadian Yacht Club; King Edward VII the Royal Lifesaving Society of Canada; King George V blessed the Royal Ottawa Sanatorium, the Royal Canadian Mounted Police, and the Royal Ontario Museum; King George VI honoured Toronto's Royal Conservatory of Music and Royal Canadian Sea Cadets. Which brings us to his daughter, Queen Elizabeth II, who has given over forty Canadian civilian and military institutions her royal wave of approval. ➤

"The long winter is an incubator for culture, and Winnipeg has always punched above its weight when it comes to culture," he explains. He credits this to the city being a "polyglot of the North," a fusion of cultures, with a strong European influence.

Fair enough, says I, but that could describe Toronto, Vancouver, or Montreal. Perhaps the answer lies in the fact that two out of every three people who see the Royal Winnipeg Ballet do so outside Winnipeg. As a financial necessity, the RWB began touring the world in the 1950s. The result is that many people's first exposure to ballet came through this company, which pirouetted in popularity in the ensuing decades. The Winnipeg Ballet got its Royal designation in 1953, the only one of its kind in Canada, and is today the longest continuously operating ballet company in North America. Not New York. Not Chicago. Spearheaded by artistic director Arnold Spohr, who guided the RWB for three decades, its program has always leaned on the populist side — something classic, something modern, and something for guys like me. I'm not familiar with the technical genius at work, but I can appreciate something beautiful when I look at it.

So, if the Royal Winnipeg Ballet is so well-received outside Winnipeg, having performed in 573 cities worldwide, why bother seeing it in its hometown?

"We're always in context in the Prairies, the colour, the light," says Jeff. "This is where we hold our world premieres and perform full sets with the Winnipeg Symphony, our home orchestra."

In hockey terms, these are the home games, with home-ice advantage. This is best illustrated in the annual free performance at the outdoor Lyric Theatre in Winnipeg's Assiniboine Park. An institution since the 1970s, the event is perfect for those who want to experience ballet in a relaxed environment. Pull up a blanket, indulge with cheese and wine from the cooler, and sit back and watch one of the world's best ballet companies dazzle an appreciative audience with a diverse selection of performances. Whether you're into the *bras croisé* or just the bodies, the Royal Winnipeg Ballet presents a distinctly Canadian cultural spectacle, for wives *and* their husbands.

START HERE: canadianbucketlist.com/ballet

CATFISH ON THE RED RIVER

If you think pike resemble fearsome prehistoric monsters, wait until you encounter the formidable channel catfish that trawl the bottom of the Red River. Each summer, fishing guides at City Cats will take you out on the river, using onboard GPS to find the creatures lurking below. Averaging seven kilograms each, all you need to do to declare yourself a master angler on the Red River is hook a thirty-four-incher (86.5 centimetres). Given the abundance of cats in the channel, this is not as rare an event as it would seem, but that doesn't mean it's easy. My first catch of the day was seventy-one centimetres. Reeling it in, I literally pulled a muscle in my groin before inventing a creative technique that involved jamming the rod in the bend of my chair. Beyond their girth and weight, catfish put up a tremendous fight. I heed the sound advice of Manitoban outdoor expert Shel Zolkewich:

↑

MANITOBA

Step One: Listen to your guide.

Step Two: Put on your big girl panties and suck it up.

Step Three: Reel in that cat, and hold on.

Muscles burning, I finally get the slippery beast to the boat, where my guide Cameron scoops it up with a net, measures it, and hands it over for my prerequisite proof-of-conquest photo. Catfish over nine kilograms are protected in the Red River. I respectfully release the beast back into the muddy river, to grow into an even bigger monster for others to enjoy.

START HERE: canadianbucketlist.com/catfish

VISIT A TROPICAL BEACH

As a travel journalist, I receive over a dozen press releases each day asserting the outstanding qualities of destinations, often from countries claiming to have it all. Well, as large as Canada is, we do have to face some facts. We don't have jungles or savannahs or large salt deserts, and as anyone who has been to the Caribbean will tell you, nor do we have tropical white-sand beaches. Unless, and somewhat bizarrely, you live in southern Manitoba. Here you'll find the cocaine-powder sand of the suitably named Grand Beach on the eastern shore of Lake Winnipeg.

Less than a ninety-minute drive from Winnipeg, I admit I have my doubts. This is the prairie, after all, and comparing a lake beach to the finest sands of Belize, Brazil, and Barbados is a mighty bold statement. Yet that's what Winnipeggers are apt to do. As the car makes its way along the flattest of highways and through the sleepy town of Grand Marais, I brush up on the grand history of Grand Beach.

In 1916, the Canadian Northern Railway opened a line connecting the town, and adjacent Victoria Beach, to the boom town of Winnipeg. With a boardwalk, shops, and the largest dance hall in the British Empire, each summer tens of thousands flocked daily to the sunny, sandy shores of Lake Winnipeg. Eight trains a day, packed to the rafters, depositing passengers on this unlikely beach of dreams.

I pop in for breakfast with Ken and Luise Avery , who have been living in Grand Marais for thirty years, running their lovely B&B, Inn Among the Oaks. With the wind blowing in a sweet fragrance from the garden, Ken fills me in on the history of the area, handing me a

A "Heck" of a Provincial Park

Named by settlers in 1876 after a volcano in Iceland, Hecla Island is surrounded by the waters of Lake Winnipeg. For almost a century, Icelandic arrivals did their best to establish a permanent settlement here, eventually moving on when neither commercial fishing nor farming proved sustainable. In its place, the provincial government established Hecla-Grindstone Provincial Park, comprised of Hecla, surrounding islands, and the adjacent peninsula. A causeway replaced the ferry service in the 1970s, and today the park is a popular summer escape. It is home to 180 species of bird and a who's who of Canadian wildlife: moose, wolf, coyote, fox, beaver, black bear, lynx, and white-tailed deer. Beyond these natural attractions is the historic Hecla Village, which includes a fishing museum, replica houses and school, a restored community hall, a log house, and a general store. Pick some wild raspberries, take a walk on the beach, play a round of golf, or take a boat ride on one of the world's largest freshwater lakes. Once you cross the causeway, you leave the grind behind. ➤

book with sepia photos recording a glorious yesteryear. One picture shows the beach and water so packed with people it's hard to distinguish the beach from the bodies. When the dance hall burned to the ground in 1950, and Winnipeg's boom began to dim, the railway discontinued their service and the area declined, until the province bought the land and turned it into Grand Beach Provincial Park in 1961.

Today's Grand Beach may not have the Atlantic City–like draw of its heyday, but it still attracts thousands of sun worshippers in the summer, particularly on weekends. When Winnipeggers strip off their layers of winter, they're a good-looking bunch, too. No less an authority than *Playboy* magazine named Grand Beach one of its "Top 10 Beaches in the World." There's still a boardwalk, a campground, a couple of flea-market stalls, and popular hiking, biking, and birdwatching trails (Grand Beach is home to several pairs of the endangered piping plover). Warm water and strong winds attract kitesurfers from around the world. "Why be pickled in salt water when you can have white sand with a freshwater lake?" Ken says, laughing.

I bid the Averys farewell, envious of their indoor hot tub, and drive to the beach itself. On their advice, I head to the fourth parking lot, keeping the sand dunes, some as high as twelve metres, on my left. It's a scorching summer day, but it's early, before the crowds show up. At this point, I confess, I'm still dubious. I've been to some of the best beaches in the world, on six continents, and with no disrespect to the locals, this is a lake beach. So what if the lake is the sixth largest in North America?

Well, I should know better by now. Grand Beach lives up to its reputation. Talcum white, it squeaks when I walk, the sand as fine and white as any tropical beach I have seen. It stretches for three kilometres, cradled by lapping water and sand dunes, a pleasant breeze blowing onshore. Day trippers begin to arrive with their umbrellas, beach balls, and sand buckets. Who can blame them? Canada may not have the world's best beaches, but with our slice of paradise in the Prairies, we've definitely got one that is unique.

START HERE: canadianbucketlist.com/grandbeach

FEEL THE CRYSTAL MENTHOL

Several years ago I was in Finland investigating a story about saunas. The Finns take the sauna ritual very seriously, so much so that they invented the word. The sauna is a place to relax, to reconnect, to cleanse, and to meditate. The heat itself is a spirit, called the *löyly*, which is to be admired and respected, discussed and adjusted. I entered a traditional smoke sauna outside of Rovaniemi, just shy of the Arctic Circle, and I melted inside a public sauna in Helsinki, where old naked men sat high on benches, enduring heat intense enough to burn the tongue of Beelzebub. (Finns use another word, *sisu*, to describe the inner strength and courage one possesses, presumably in order to survive a public sauna.) I expected that was to be my most intense sauna experience, but that was before I visited Thermëa, a spa complex in Winnipeg. The spa is owned by the same company that owns Nordik Spa-Nature, the largest Nordic-inspired spa in North America, located in Gatineau,

Quebec. These are people dedicated to the art of relaxing, and their latest complex is just gorgeous.

Bring forth the eucalyptus and orange steam rooms, pools of varying temperatures, relaxation rooms with headphones and ergonomic heated benches, an on-site restaurant, and a host of massage treatments. Nordic spas want you to heat up and cool off in succession, recharging your senses, delivering a range of benefits. Let us remove our robes and take the top bench in the Finlandia sauna, authentic enough to bring a tear of sweat to any Finn's eye. Although it is winter and pushing −30°C outside, my spells in the steam rooms and pools make the cold inconsequential. Sure, if I had long hair, I might have been able to pull off a frozen-hair pic, but this is a place to relax, not win the Internet. A towelled sauna master invites everyone to take a seat on the wooden benches. He advises us to simply walk out of the room if it gets too intense. Hey pal, I got flogged with birch branches in a Siberian sauna and stared down the scrotum of a Finnish grandpa in Helsinki. I can take it!

"Today, we are going to use crystal menthol," he explains. I'm not sure what that is exactly, but it's got a damn fine name, nonetheless.

Placing perfectly round balls of snow on the rocks, the sauna master adds a spoonful of tincture to the balls and flattens them with a wooden spoon. Next, he ceremonially waves a towel, distributing the heat around the room. When it hits me, combined with the intense menthol rush of the essence, it grips my lungs in a chokehold. Eyes burning, I have to go deep within myself and find my *sisu*, and when I do, the *löyly* kicks the crap out of it. It is intense, it is a rush, and it is incredible. The bucket list is all about chasing unique moments of magic, moments that stay with you for the rest of your life. How amazing would a sauna have to be to make it one of those moments? Thermëa amazing.

Once the sauna is over, I get to relax in the hot pools outside, overcome with a sense of relaxation, of cleanliness, of sound mind and body. Hot damn! That Thermëa experience took me places; a hot rush of cool crystal menthol to the head.

START HERE: canadianbucketlist.com/thermea

HAVE A HAPPY FOLK FESTIVAL

The Winnipeg Folk Festival is one of the world's most popular music festivals, a bold statement backed up by its enduring legacy, its global reputation, and the participatory nature of the community to which it belongs. A local named Don Greig, visiting for his thirty-seventh year, puts it succinctly: "There are comfort foods, and what we have here is comfort entertainment." Bea Cherniak, here on her thirty-ninth consecutive visit, typically hates crowds, but she loves the fest. "It's gotten bigger over the years, sure, but its heart is still Folk Fest."

The heart of which she speaks takes no time seducing me. As I walk around the nine stages, meeting areas, food lanes, beer tents, and campgrounds, the atmosphere is enchantingly welcoming. Strangers greet each other with big smiles and a "Happy Folk Fest!" The sound of acoustic instruments — guitar, horns, strings, even piano — permeates the air. There are 2,950 volunteers donating a combined 55,000 hours of their time to make it happen, directed by just fifty full- and part-time and contract employees. Volunteers share the backstage tent with the performers, all fed by a volunteer-staffed kitchen that produces more than nine-thousand meals a day. Every effort is made to recycle, following a model green policy that keeps the grounds of Birds Hill Provincial Park in immaculate shape over the five-day event. Of the roughly sixteen-thousand people who visit each day, six thousand will be camping on-site on grounds that have turned into a destination unto themselves.

The camping atmosphere here is so fun, inviting, and creative that I easily understand why some campers don't even make it to the main stages. Festival-supported animation areas allow amateur musicians to perform, while others can rest in hammocks, drum in tipis, play giant board games, dress up, and join jolly daily parades. I pitch my tent with the Castle Boys, a dozen guys and girls with a reputation for throwing the wildest parties and building the most striking installations. It's difficult to tear myself away from their party and make the ten-minute walk to the main grounds. The festival also offers an RV and caravan section, along with a Quiet Camping Ground better suited for families.

Although it is much smaller in scale, the Folk Fest embodies a spirit I first discovered at Burning Man, a massive cultural event in the Black Rock Desert in Nevada. A feeling that makes you believe in humanity and goodwill, and that everything is going to turn out just fine after all. I tell a reporter it feels like Burning Man in the

TRADING POST 203m

CAMPGROUND CENTRAL 264m

560m

GENERAL STORE

FIRST AID 298m

ENVIRO HQ 240m

HANDMADE VILLAGE

PARIS 6610 Km

Feeling folky in Saskatchewan? First held in 1969, the Regina Folk Festival is the longest-running music festival in the Prairies, and in all of Western Canada, for that matter. Attracting some twenty thousand people, the festival takes place in Regina's Victoria Park each August. ➤

Prairies and am surprised to see my quote on the front page of the *Winnipeg Free Press* the following day.

As much fun as the camping is (the limited spaces sell out quickly), performances by some of the best musicians on the planet are still the primary draw. Under the clear prairie sky, sweetened with the tang of a tangerine sunset, I watch as singer-songwriters capture the audience's attention with their songcraft, politically minded lyrics, and simple charisma. The weather is smashing, and with the successful introduction of mosquito-chomping dragonflies, Manitoba's legendary summer biting insects are blessedly absent. An eight-piece Latin band kicks up the energy, the music swinging from salsa to jazz to pop to soul. With more than seventy acts, the organizers ensure there is something for everyone. Unique to the Winnipeg Folk Fest, many of these artists will also collaborate through improvised workshop performances on the day stages, leading to some of the best musical experiences of the entire event.

K'naan, a Somali-born Canadian rapper-poet, rocks the crowd and wraps up the main concert, but the party continues until way after sunrise, especially atop Pope's Hill. It was built by the Catholic Church for the 1984 visit of Pope John Paul II, but I enjoyed its reincarnation as a venue for watching dreadlocked drummers beat tribal rhythms as thousands dance and drink in the new day. Not quite the spiritual communion the hill was built for, but for many it's an ecstatic religious experience nonetheless.

Canadian summers are a time for outdoor celebration. The folk festivals of Edmonton, Vancouver, Yellowknife, and Regina do an incredible job allowing people of all ages and musical tastes to come together, listen, party, interact, and get involved. Winnipeg, that beating heart of culture in the middle of Canada, hosts the granddaddy of them all. Leaving Birds Hill Provincial Park for the short drive back to the city, I tell the Castle Boys I'll be back, with a lot more folks in tow.

START HERE: canadianbucketlist.com/folkfest

PADDLE A BLOODY RIVER

A three-hundred-kilometre-long river that flows through unspoilt virgin boreal forest and is called the Bloodvein conjures up strong images of violence. Its name may refer to a bloody skirmish between local First Nations tribes, or simply to the veins that can be seen in the ancient red granite rocks and riverbed. Either way, rafting or canoeing down this remote Canadian Heritage River is an adventure that paddles (and portages) its way onto our bucket list.

Rafters take anywhere from a week to fifteen days to complete the journey, with some choosing to floatplane in and out of certain lakes, carrying in all their gear as there is no road access. The Bloodvein corridor is a series of pools and drops, and as a result can be tackled in either direction, although most paddlers will go with the flow to exit at the Narrows on Lake Winnipeg, about two hundred kilometres northeast of Winnipeg. The river favours those paddlers with experience. There are more than a hundred rapids, unmarked and wild enough to send you downriver on the wrong side of the canoe. Reading whitewater is a handy skill, one you'll almost certainly have developed by the final stroke.

Glaciers scoured the area during the last ice age, and due to its inaccessibility, the Bloodvein was not used for trade or settlement. The result is virgin landscape, full of old-growth forest and wildlife that fulfill the promise of the Great Outdoors. Marshes, forests, lakes, and the ancient rocks of the Canadian Shield host an abundance of animals, several of which are rare and endangered. Besides the usual suspects — black bears, moose, deer, otters, beavers — you're in the domain of wolverines, great grey owls, white osprey, and woodland caribou. Surrounding you is some of the oldest rock on the planet, and beneath you swim trophy-size northern pike, walleye, lake trout, and sturgeon. During your paddle you'll also see signs of ancient human history, archaeological sites from hunter-gatherers dating back six thousand years, and red-ochre pictographs in Artery Lake drawn between CE 900 and 1200. The Ojibwa people did use the river as a trapping area, and their descendants still live in the community of Bloodvein, at the mouth of the river, operating a lodge that greets paddlers at the end of their journey.

Paddlers will tackle the river from spring until fall, with July and August being the most popular months. That being said, you won't find that the campsites located on the spits and shores of Atikaki Provincial Wilderness Park and Ontario's adjacent Woodland Caribou Provincial Wilderness Park are crowded. There are no facilities or services, and the remoteness that has largely protected the Bloodvein from human history will continue to reserve it for those seeking a water-bound wilderness experience. Fortunately, guided tours are available to help us novices navigate the river channels, the whitewater, and the challenges of a multi-day canoe trip. For a name steeped in blood and battles, the Bloodvein offers just the sort of rugged adventure by which to experience the true peace of nature.

START HERE: canadianbucketlist.com/bloodvein

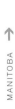

STAND BENEATH A POLAR BEAR

Churchill hogs Canada's polar bear glory, although not everyone has the time or the resources to hop aboard a tundra buggy. Fortunately, there's another polar bear experience in Manitoba that can scratch your *ursus maritimus* itch. The not-for-profit organization that runs Assiniboine Park, a sprawling 160-hectare park on the shores of the Assiniboine River, spent $90 million on the Arctic enclosure and Polar Bear Conservation Centre at its popular zoo. Part of an extensive $200-million upgrade over ten years, the zoo has become a world-class fixture for anyone hoping to connect with the great animals of the north: wolves, snowy owls, Arctic fox, moose, cougars, elk, caribou, and, of course, polar bears.

Residing along a scenic walkway called "The Journey to Churchill," animals might live in large enclosures, but they still stop visitors in their tracks. Several readers might feel queasy about animals in captivity. Think about this: all but one of the six polar bears at Assiniboine Park was rescued from the Churchill wilds (the other was born in captivity). A fed bear is a dead bear, and so is a cub abandoned by its mother. Whether you believe the bear should have

died in the wild or is better off being fed and nurtured in a zoo is a matter of personal taste. My own thoughts: A well-run zoo plays a vital role in the conservation of wildlife, serving as a crucial tool in our education and interaction with species we share this planet with. Nature documentaries are wonderful, but observing an animal in the flesh makes them real. Critical to my bold statement is the adjective *well-run*. Bruised in my memory is a visit to Cairo Zoo many years ago, where I had the misfortune to see polar bears locked in a tiny, filthy enclosure and elephants chained to a stump. Outraged, I wrote a letter to the World Wildlife Fund to protest these conditions, knowing my verbiage would make scant difference. But that was a world away from Winnipeg, where the enclosures are spacious and the animals seem to be treated better than household pets. There's enough space for bison to chase each other around, and wolves to disappear over the hill. Clearly, the animal's comfort and health is of primary concern. I believe we easily succumb to anthropomorphism

— attributing human qualities to animals that don't have them. Would a polar bear be happier in the wild, battling each day for survival in a constant struggle for food? Is that fed bear/wolf/moose happier in the zoo? Can a moose be happy in the first place? Until we start talking to the animals, like Dr. Doolittle, we can't say for sure. In the meantime, the animals, of Winnipeg look healthy and content. There's no denying the contentment of visitors when they enter the Arctic Centre to find themselves standing beneath a pair of swimming polar bears. The three-metre-wide, six-inch-thick transparent acrylic tunnel puts an O-ring on the mouths of believers and opponents alike. Polar bears are stunning to observe on land. Wait until you see them gracefully gliding underwater or resting their powerful paws just above your head. With their creamy, off-white hair bristling like an aquatic hairbrush, never have polar bears appeared so charming, magical, and accessible. It makes you want to know more about their habits, their habitats, and the challenges they are facing due

to climate change. Information is offered through the excellent use of interactive displays and interpretation boards. As for the bears, they interact when they feel like it, though they are particularly active in the winter months, when Winnipeg's climate more closely resembles that of Churchill. For those heading to Churchill, a visit to Assiniboine Park is a fantastic introduction/epilogue to the world of Arctic wildlife. For the rest of us, and families in particular, it's a marvellous day out on the Prairies Bucket List.

START HERE: canadianbucketlist.com/assiniboine

HÉ HO TO THE VOYAGEURS!

A solemn candlelight procession departs from the Canadian Museum for Human Rights. It doesn't take long for the icy whipping wind to extinguish my flame, which I tried pitifully to protect with a plastic cup. Hundreds of people continue across the Esplanade Riel, right at Tache Avenue, shuddering forward beneath the old ruins of the original St. Boniface Cathedral. As church bells chime, we pay homage at the gravesite of Louis Riel before continuing on toward Voyageur Park. Even if the temperature has dipped below minus forty degrees Celsius with the wind chill, and even if I am still coming to grips with Prairie French-Canadian and Métis culture, it is an earnest bucket list moment. Best of all, we're just

moments away from the fireworks show that will signify the start of the Festival du Voyageur, the largest winter carnival in the Prairies.

With long days and backbreaking work in an environment as hospitable as a rabid python, the voyageurs paddled their way into Canadian lore as the toughest of men. Organized fur traders for the Northwest Company (a fierce competitor of the Hudson's Bay Company before being swallowed by it), these rugged French-Canadian woodsmen had a reputation for hardiness, industriousness, and a certain *joie de vivre*. In the early nineteenth century, these men canoed down raging rivers transporting the furs from the animals they'd trapped up north to trading posts in the south. Eventually, these adventurous voyageurs were phased out with the

The Heart of the Nation?

Manitobans are proud of the fact that their province is at the geographical heart of Canada — although, technically speaking, that's not the case. It does sit at the longitudinal centre of the country, but the place located directly between the most northerly and southerly points of Canada, and between the country's most easterly and westerly points, is a little town called Arviat, in the Northwest Territories. ➤

invention of the railway and the decreasing demand for furs, but their legacy lives on with their descendants, the Métis nation, celebrated during this vibrant ten-day annual festival.

Winnipeg's St. Boniface boasts the largest French-speaking community west of Quebec. Each February, the neighbourhood's Voyageur Park attracts hundreds of thousands of revellers with music performances, contests, parades, food stands, and family-friendly activities. Having warmed my blood up with a sweet, fortified beverage called *caribou* (served in an ice glass), I find myself in the main tent eating poutine, chewing on freshly poured maple taffy, and foot-stomping along to a jig. A terrific band called The Dead South take the stage with a now-familiar greeting of "Hé Ho!" — the festival's boisterous rallying cry. I didn't think it possible for the temperature to drop more, but that isn't stopping the ice sculptors scraping the finishing touches into their creations outside, or the lineup of people waiting to get into the tent. Voyageurs playing a game of Nine Men's Morris in their trading posts would have been proud.

Fort Gibraltar was a fur-trading post originally built in 1810 at The Forks — the point where the Red and Assiniboine rivers meet. It has been impressively reconstructed upriver in Voyageur Park as a living historical site, complete with costumed actors recounting tales from the daily lives of the voyageurs. For these men, no portage was too long, no dried pemmican too foul, and no bag of fur too heavy, even for the pittance they received in return, which was barely a living wage. The spartan living conditions at the trading posts were reminiscent of prisons. Through trading and intermarriage with Aboriginal populations along the trading routes, the voyageurs ultimately helped to create the Métis nation, effectively establishing the province of Manitoba.

Outside the fort, artists from ten countries admire their snow sculptures, sparkling in the morning sun. I strap on snowshoes for a guided walk along the Red River, but ditch them later for a thrilling toboggan track. Activity tents provide suitable refuge from the chill, but locals are only proving what I've long believed: you can't do Canada if you can't do cold.

While their role in society was phased out, the voyageurs' ability to enjoy life in any conditions has surely been passed down to their descendants. How else can you explain the festive atmosphere and outdoor carnival spirit when Winnipeg's thermometer falls below "my nose is an ice sculpture" level? No matter how cold it gets, bundle up for the maple taffy, snow cones, flapjacks, and festivities. And if the lineup gets too long, draw on the spirit of the voyageur (and put some toe warmers in your boots).

START HERE: canadianbucketlist.com/voyageur

THE FORKS FOR ALL SEASONS

There are several urban markets in the Prairies — the farmers' markets in Saskatoon and Regina come to mind — but only one of them can claim six thousand years of Aboriginal history and has been designated a National Historic Site. The first time I explored The Forks, it was during a short stopover on VIA Rail's Canadian, as I journeyed by train from Vancouver to Toronto. I liked the market, but was more struck by the physical meeting of the mighty Assiniboine and Red Rivers. It is a junction that long ago attracted hunters, traders, pioneers, and settlers, while today it attracts tourists hunting for souvenirs and residents hunting for local gourmet treats. There's also a theatre,

POP IN TO A POP-UP RESTAURANT

Each winter, at the convergence of Winnipeg's frozen Red and Assiniboine Rivers, Raw: Almond emerges atop the ice to offer a true bucket list dining experience. The brainchild of two chefs and a gallery director, the idea was to "pop-up" a temporary restaurant directly on the river, collaborating with the city's best chefs and celebrating the essence of winter through inspired food and design. Sitting on a log just steps away from the bustling kitchen radiating tantalizing aromas, I feast on duck confit and goat perogies while slow sipping vodka from an ice glass: a memorable pairing if ever there was one. You'll need to reserve well in advance, though, for one of the coolest dinners in Canada. ➤

children's museum, boutique hotel, a tourism exhibit, and it is only a short walk from here to the Canadian Museum for Human Rights (see page 122).

When the Assiniboine freezes over during the winter, out come the skating trails, Olympic-sized ice rinks, and beautifully designed warming huts. Winter also brings with it pop-up restaurants and ice sculptures, and as the temperature plummeted to minus thirty degrees during one of my visits, it reaffirmed my belief that you can't experience the best of Canada if you can't take the cold. Just make sure you're dressed for it!

Whatever the season, Parks Canada operates an area adjacent to The Forks that has walking trails, a prairie garden, an outdoor amphitheatre, and a canoe beach. The Oodena Celebration Circle, with its eight steel arms pointing toward

specific constellations, is another visitor highlight. Since that first train stop, I've visited Winnipeg on many occasions, and each time I return, I inevitably find myself at The Forks, enjoying some aspect of it I did not discover the last time round. New exhibitions, art, food, and culture, all can be found at the very confluence of Manitoba's rich history.

START HERE: canadianbucketlist.com/theforks

RIDE IN TO RIDING MOUNTAIN

Located on the escarpment in south-central Manitoba, Riding Mountain National Park is a three-thousand-kilometre green lung of parkland and boreal forest surrounded by prairie farm-land. It is the only road-accessible national park in the province. Recognized by UNESCO as a biosphere reserve, there's camp-ing, resorts, and inns in Wasagaming (also known as Clear Lake), including Parks Canada's hybrid tent/cabin, the A-frame oTENTik.

MANITOBA ↑

Come for the trails, come for the wildlife (Riding Mountain is one of the best parks to encounter the great animals of the north), or come for the cinnamon buns at the Whitehouse Bakery, which have no equal in the nation.

START HERE: canadianbucketlist.com/ridingmountain

HOOK A SMALLMOUTH BASS

Our floatplane takes off as I hold my cup of piping hot coffee.

According to my friend Scott, an editor at *Outdoor Canada*, that opening sentence right there is your typical cliché for any remote fishing lodge story. Since I'm no angler journalist, I figure I'll stick with it. Only there is no piping hot coffee, and I am breaking speed limits I shouldn't be in a Ford F-150 rocketing across the flat Manitoban prairies en route to Adventure Air in Lac du Bonnet. Through fate and circumstance, I have been invited to Eagle Nest Lodge, a fly-in fishing lodge on the Winnipeg River. At this point, I should note that I did indeed hold a cup of piping hot coffee as the floatplane took off.

My previous fishing experience included:

- Hooking a barracuda and wahoo in the Cook Islands.
- Hooking dying sockeye salmon on a river in Alaska.
- Hooking piranha in Venezuela and Brazil.

Barracuda tasted best; the piranha was way too bony. The pursuit of trophy fish is a serious business, and much like jocks and football players, anglers judge one another by the size and weight of their tackle. The abundant waters of the Winnipeg River, cutting channels through hundreds of islands, are a world-class fishing destination. Eagle Nest, a family-owned lodge in operation since 1966, offers eighteen staff for its forty guests, serviced by two-dozen boats, fully equipped cabins, gourmet meals, and hard-won knowledge on the best spots to hook the local attractions: smallmouth bass, northern pike, walleye, sauger, perch, and, to a lesser extent, sturgeon.

Fred Pedruchny, who took the lodge over from his parents in 1977, and has been here every summer since, tells me the largest pike caught in these waters was a fifty-inch monster. But it's not just about catching fish. Escaping the city, being in the wilderness, hanging out with friends and family — this is Manitoban wilderness, where at any point you'll be at least an hour's boat ride (or twenty-minute floatplane ride) from anywhere.

Jason, one of the sun-bronzed fishing guides, says there are only two things you need to pack when you go fishing: a raincoat and sunglasses. When it rains, the water whips across our boat. In the sun, my fair skin sizzles. Rain or shine, mosquitoes and horse flies are determined to take their pound of flesh.

In the capable hands of the fishing guides and far more experienced fishing buddies, it takes no time before I catch my first walleye. Sport fishing is strictly catch and release, but we are allowed to hold on to a right-sized walleye for our shore lunch. Pike's flesh is not as desirable,

so we throw them back, even the ones large enough to feed half of North Korea.

I learn to jig, cast, and troll. Comedian Demetri Martin was right: fishing *should* be called tricking and killing. Or tricking and letting go. There's a healthy respect here for the fish: barbs are pinched to minimize physical damage. My trophy of the day is a thirty-one-inch (seventy-eight-centimetre) pike. Despite my inexperience, I haul in several species of fish, including a healthy sized and much-prized smallmouth bass. Trust me, this says more about the number of fish in the Winnipeg River than about my fishing skills.

In the early afternoon, we all gather on an island for lunch, our guides making short work filleting the fish, which are rubbed in spice or dunked in flour and cornflakes, deep-fried, and served with fire-roasted potatoes. Fish, to me, has never tasted better, or fresher.

As one of the world's largest flowing rivers (by volume), the Winnipeg River boasts abundance. An abundance of water, clean enough for hardier anglers to drink and warm enough for late afternoon dips. An abundance of fish. An abundance of good times. Eagles fly overhead; mink, bear, and deer roam the shores. Casting off the dock with my new fishing buddies at sunset, I share Fred's sentiment: for all its tall tales and trophies, fishing is something to keep you busy while you ponder life with good friends under an enormous prairie sky.

START HERE: canadianbucketlist.com/eaglenest

does one move beyond injustice, transcend revenge, and avoid the yo-yo of hate that has plagued society's evolution? Given the exposed nerves bleeding between these and many other questions, any space that encourages such conversation is bound to feel the hot breath of controversy.

Bundled in layers against the icy chill of winter, I walk into Winnipeg's most striking building somewhat apprehensive. Would this be a holier-than-thou exhibition in a country, indeed a city, with a history of Aboriginal conflict? How can a museum possibly encapsulate everything from the horrors of genocide to gay rights? I check my expectations in with my coat, and begin in the dark and cavernous Bonnie and John Buhler Hall.

Ambitious in scope, bewildering in budget, outstanding in execution — the Canadian Museum for Human Rights is the first national museum built outside the capital region of Ottawa. First conceived by media mogul Izzy Asper as a museum to celebrate tolerance, it took fifteen years and $351 million in private sector, federal, and provincial money before the doors opened to the public in late 2014. Based on the ambitious designs of American architect Antoine Predock, construction costs spiked higher than its twenty-three-storey Tower of Hope. Then the 2008 recession bit as viciously as a winter wind blasting down the Red River. Predock's unusual design and his insistence on using Manitoban stone and glass, Spanish alabaster, Mongolian basalt, and white-painted steel ignited the critics, creating construction nightmares. Then — despite the efforts of history and human rights academics and extensive public engagement — came the protests: Why a permanent exhibit about the Holocaust and not the Holodomor? When discussing cultural genocide, there was a demand by Aboriginal leaders to include Canada's treatment of its First Nations. Reassuringly, a museum that celebrates the positive power of protests welcomed the debate, fully aware its curators will never be able to please everybody.

I walk up the first in a series of seemingly endless glowing ramps to the first gallery, a stunning space that explores the concept, history,

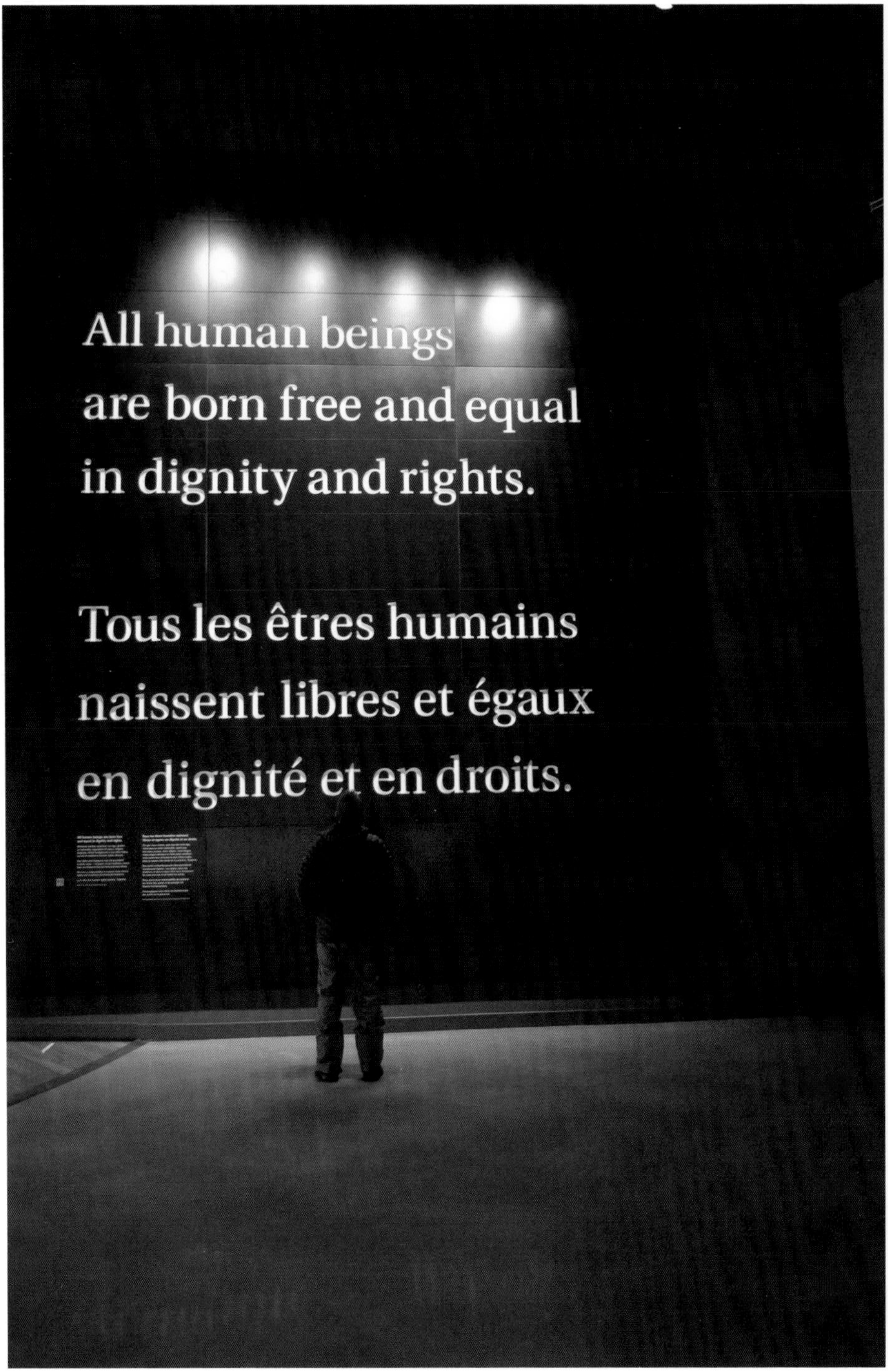
All human beings
are born free and equal
in dignity and rights.
Tous les êtres humains
naissent libres et égaux
en dignité et en droits.

Facts About the CMHR

- The CMHR is the first new Canadian national museum built since 1967.
- On the grounds, fifteen species of prairie grasses create the largest urban installation of natural, original vegetation in the country.
- There are seven theatres, an immersive multimedia experience, 360-degree film, and two soundscapes.
- Visitors explore the galleries along eight hundred metres of glowing ramps made of Spanish alabaster, symbolizing a path of light through darkness. It will take a fit person about thirty minutes to walk the ramps.
- The eleven galleries sit within a "mountain" of 400-million-year-old limestone, surrounded by a glass "cloud" of 1,300 panes, with no two exactly the same.
- The CMHR is the same size and has been compared to the Guggenheim Museum, Bilbao, in Spain.
- More than 80 percent of the building's walls are sloped at unusual angles, making its geometrical and spatial structure unique in Canada.
- The CMHR is located on First Nations Treaty One land, a meeting place for thousands of years. The museum funded an archaeological excavation that recovered more than four hundred thousand artifacts. ➤

and value of human rights. It is easy to see how the millions were spent. Exhibits here and throughout the museum use state-of-the-art technology to create an immersive multimedia experience. There are hundreds of video clips and thousands of images, most of which are accessed through interactive tablets inviting personal investigation. A 360-degree theatre shows a short film about Aboriginal perspectives, leading to "Canadian Journeys," the largest gallery in the museum. Stations along the rim of the large hall reveal all aspects of human rights in Canada's history. Gay marriage is celebrated with a chandelier of moving wedding photos, selected from thousands solicited from the public. I learn about the fight for language rights, religious rights, gender quality, disability rights, residential schools, and workers' rights. A large group of children are being guided in the centre of the room, interacting on a digital canvas. While many battles are still being fought, in Canada and around the world, each

station represents a victory. Each station suggests these kids are now growing up in a better world.

Glowing alabaster ramps continue to the next level, looking like a science-fiction movie set. Indeed, I expect it is only a matter of time before Hollywood arrives to take advantage of these distinctly futuristic walkways. Just how controversial human rights can be is explored in an interactive exhibit that lets visitors vote on Supreme Court decisions. Should a young Sikh boy be allowed to carry a ceremonial knife to school? After explaining the arguments, it's no easy decision. A real-time poll shows that 60 percent of today's visitors had voted yes, 40 percent no.

Level Four's permanent exhibition on the Holocaust is outstanding. As a Jew — as a human — the subject is deeply personal, evoking complex emotions of rage, pain, sadness, and vengefulness. Having visited Holocaust museums in New York, Jerusalem, and Berlin, as well as Auschwitz in Poland, it is still impossible to grasp the scale of this genocide. Some museums use symbolic art. Others use shocking footage. The central display here focuses on complicity, the brutal fact that the Nazi's industrial killing machine needed accountants and secretaries and architects. It asks: Are *we* complicit in today's atrocities? Are we also just going with the flow, following orders, believing what we're told? This leads us to a gallery entitled "Breaking the Silence," which examines genocides throughout history. A large digital display case lets me scroll through the ages, examining the causes, evidence, and result of mankind's darkest hours. One can spend hours in this room alone. Having learned about the horrors, we now move on to "Hope": life-sized digital displays introducing individuals whose actions have changed the course of history: Ghandi, King, Mandela, Suu Kyi, Malala, and many others whom you might not have heard of. A bold display showcases the Universal Declaration of Human Rights, and we ramp up to the final floor, which showcases the complexity, challenges, and heroes of the fight for human rights today. A glass elevator shepherds me to the late Izzy Asper's Tower of Hope, and grants those ascending a view of the open-plan offices of the researchers, curators, and academics who work to keep the museum current, while using it as a beacon for human rights across the globe.

I meet some friends back on level three amidst the pillars, pools, and glass of the Garden of Contemplation. Prairie sunlight bathes us through the glass walls and sky-high ceiling. We have an earnest discussion about our experience, a need to make sense of it all. Some feel the technology and architecture got in the way. Others were moved to tears. We all agree that the Canadian Museum for Human Rights is more than just a museum. It is more than the legacy of a media mogul or hubris of a rock star architect, and more than just the most striking building in the Prairies. On a personal level, visitors of all ages and backgrounds might connect with the space, the stories, the art, and the technology. They will surely connect with the message. For while some exhibits reveal the horrors of humanity at its worst, this is a space reassuringly infused with hope. Despite controversies that have plagued its development and content, the mere existence of the CMHR speaks volumes about

the desire of Canada to transcend its own sordid history. It proudly declares that vital conversations must continue to take place, and that they can start right here in the Prairies. Most of all, it is a strikingly physical reminder that if we don't learn from the mistakes of our past, we are forever doomed to repeat them.

START HERE: canadianbucketlist.com/cmhr

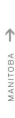

EPILOGUE

My travels have allowed me to learn a thing or two: the importance of smiling and not panicking in tricky situations; trusting my instincts; keeping an open mind; remembering to check my expectations with my baggage. But perhaps the most important nugget of wisdom is, it's the people we meet who create the paradise we find. Itineraries are an outline, but characters and personalities shade in the colours of any journey. My single biggest piece of advice when it comes to tackling any experience in this book is: share it with good people, and if you're on your own, be open and friendly to those around you.

It's also worth noting that travel is as personal as your choice of underwear. You might not meet the folks I met, have the same weather, or enjoy each experience as much as I did. Your experience of the Prairies is as unique as yourself — even if you're only reading the pages of this book.

The Great Canadian Prairies Bucket List is a terrific start, but I'm well aware there are woeful omissions, items known and less known that I haven't got to just yet. Some of them will pop up on canadianbucketlist.com, where you can also let me know what I'm missing. I expect my Canadian Bucket Lists will keep growing over the years, because the more we dig, the more we'll find, and the more we find, the more we can celebrate, sharing the best of Canada with locals and visitors alike.

Canoeing on Lac la Ronge, exploring Hecla/Grindstone Provincial Park, one-of-a-kind restaurants and hotels — there's always more to discover. Every chapter in this book concludes with two important words: **START HERE**. I'll end the book with two more: **START NOW**.

RE
robin@robinesrock.com
@robinesrock

ACKNOWLEDGEMENTS

The Great Canadian Prairies Bucket List is the result of many miles and many hours of travel, with the professional and personal help of many people and organizations. My deep gratitude to all below, along with all the airlines, ferries, trains, buses, hotels, B&B's, and organizations who helped along the way.

Saskatchewan: Tourism Saskatchewan, Jonathan Potts, Shane Owen, Jodi Holliday, Carla Bechard, Jenn Smith Nelson, Corporal Dan Toppings, the RCMP, Tyrone Tootoosis, Gord Vaaderland, Aviva Zack, Alexandra Stang, Tourism Saskatoon, Tourism Regina, Gary Kalmek, Parks Canada.

Manitoba: Travel Manitoba, Cathy Senecal, Julia Adams, Jillian Reckseidler, Linda Whitfield, Gillian Chester, Tourism Winnipeg, Tricia Schers, Lynda Gunter, Neil Mumby, Maureen Fitzhenry, Shel Zolkewich, Parks Canada, Robert and Kristen Baron.

Special Thanks: Karen McMullin, Margaret Bryant, Kirk Howard, Carrie Gleason, Allison Hirst, Synora van Drine, Courtney Horner and all at Dundurn Press. Hilary McMahon and all at Westwood Creative Artists, Cathy Hirst and all at the Lavin Agency, Jon Rothbart, Joe Kalmek, Gary Kalmek, Sean Aiken, David Rock, Heather Taylor, Guy Theriault, Jennifer Burnell, Lauren More, Josh Norton, Linda Bates, Patrick Crean, the Canadian Tourism Commission's Go Media Marketplace, Josephine Wasch, Nathalie Gauthier, Kerri May, Jarrod Levitan, Vancouver and Burnaby Public Libraries, Chris Lee, Sherill Sirrs, Mary Rostad, RtCamp, and the Kalmek and Esrock families.

Thanks to everyone who has attended one of my speaking events, and/or registered on canadianbucketlist.com.

SPECIAL THANKS TO THE FOLLOWING, WITHOUT WHOM THERE WOULD BE NO COMPANION WEBSITE OR SPEAKING TOURS:

Ford Motors Canada, Parks Canada, VIA Rail, Travel Manitoba, Tourism Saskatchewan, Tourism New Brunswick, Great Canadian Trails, and Keen Footwear.

And finally, to my parents, Joe and Cheryl Kalmek (without whom there would be no Robin Esrock), my ever-supportive wife, Ana Carolina, and my inspirational daughter, Raquel Ayla.

PHOTO CREDITS

OTHER GREAT BUCKET LIST ADVENTURE BOOKS

The Great Atlantic Canada Bucket List

Robin Esrock loves all that our eastern provinces have to offer, and so will you! Activities and destinations that might seem ho-hum to locals will amaze us "come-from-aways," whether we're driving on some of the world's most beautiful roads, catching some fresh seafood, hiking in the national parks, or discovering the region's storied history. *The Great Atlantic Canada Bucket List* highlights the best travel experiences to be had on Canada's East Coast.

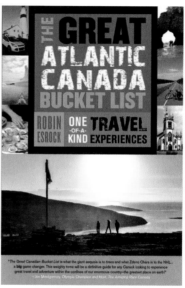

Not your typical travel guide, Robin's recommendations encompass outdoor adventure and natural wonders as well as the unique food, culture, and history of Canada's Atlantic Provinces.

Categorized by province, *The Great Atlantic Canada Bucket List* will give you a first-hand perspective on:

- Ziplining over a waterfall in New Brunswick.
- Harvesting an iceberg for a Newfoundland cocktail.
- Exploring Nova Scotia's Cabot Trail.
- Walking the seabed beneath Hopewell Rocks.
- Cycling across Prince Edward Island.
- Rafting a tidal wave in the Bay of Fundy.
- … and much more!

The Great Central Canada Bucket List

Most Canadians think of travel as a way to escape the snow, cold, and dreary winter skies. But Robin Esrock loves all that the provinces of Ontario and Quebec have to offer, and so will you! *The Great Central Canada Bucket List* highlights the best travel experiences to be had in the heart of Canada.

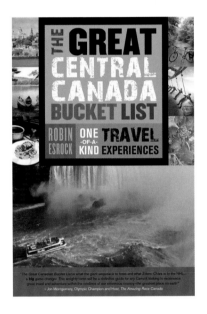

Renowned travel writer and TV host Robin Esrock explored every inch of central Canada to craft the definitive Bucket List for the region. Running the gamut of nature, food, culture, history, adrenaline rushes, and quirky Canadiana, Robin's personal quest to tick off the very best of Ontario and Quebec packs in enough for a lifetime.

Categorized by province, *The Great Central Canada Bucket List* will give you a first-hand perspective on:

- Riding a motorcycle around Lake Superior.
- Drinking *caribou* with Bonhomme.
- Unravelling a mystery in Algonquin Park.
- Spending the night at an ice hotel.
- Scaling the via ferrata at Mont-Tremblant.
- Exploring the great museums.
- Cave-swimming in the Magdalen Islands.
- … and much more!

The Great Northern Canada Bucket List

Travelling across Canada's vast northern territories, Robin Esrock was delighted to find unique adventures for both visitors and locals alike. Through his discovery of the local culture, history, food, and wilderness, and a few quirky tidbits of Canadiana, Robin's personal quest to tick off the exceptional activities of the North pack in enough adventure for a lifetime. Accompanied by recommendations, and with bonus content available online, discover one-of-a-kind experiences in Yukon, Northwest Territories, and Nunavut.

Categorized by territory, *The Great Northern Canada* Bucket List will give you a first-hand perspective on:

- Crossing the Northwest Passage.
- Camping in the High Arctic.
- Watching wild beluga whales play at your feet.
- Tasting muktuk and Arctic char.
- Dogsledding with a Yukon Quest legend.
- Flying with Buffalo Air.
- Swallowing the Sourtoe Cocktail.
- … and much more!

The Great Western Canada Bucket List

Most Canadians think of travel as a way to escape the snow, cold, and dreary winter skies. But Robin Esrock loves all that our western provinces have to offer, and so will you! *The Great Western Canada Bucket List* highlights some of the best travel experiences to be had on Canada's West Coast.

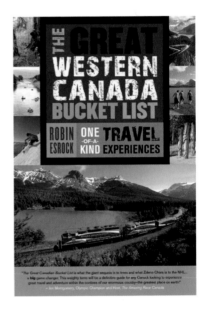

Through nature, food, culture, and history, as well as a few adrenaline rushes and some quirky Canadiana, Robin's personal quest to tick off the very best of Alberta and British Columbia packs in enough adventure for a lifetime.

Categorized by province, *The Great Western Canada Bucket List* will give you a first-hand perspective on:

- Sailing in Haida Gwaii.
- Tracking the spirit bear in B.C.'s Great Bear Rainforest.
- Wine-tasting in the Okanagan.
- Hunting for dinosaurs in Alberta's Badlands.
- Diving a sunken battleship.
- Snorkelling with salmon.
- Surviving the Calgary Stampede.
- RVing the Icefields Parkway.
- … and much more!

The Great Canadian Bucket List

Renowned travel writer and TV host Robin Esrock spent years visiting every province and territory to craft the definitive National Bucket List. Having travelled to more than one hundred countries on six continents, he never expected Canada to offer so much, and neither will you!

This isn't a typical travel guide — it is an inspiration for your next trip. Spanning the outdoors, food, culture, and history, Robin's personal journey to tick off the very best of Canada features well-known and hidden gems, and is infused with humour, trivia, advice, and unforgettable characters.

Categorized by province, *The Great Canadian Bucket List* will give you a first-hand perspective on:

- Tracking the Spirit Bear in BC's Great Bear Rainforest.
- Ziplining over a massive waterfall in New Brunswick.
- Digging for dinosaur bones in Alberta's Badlands.
- Harvesting an iceberg for a refreshing Newfoundland cocktail.
- Finding the best smoked meat sandwich in Montreal.
- Floating in Canada's very own Dead Sea.
- Cracking the nation's own Da Vinci Code in Winnipeg.
- Hiking the tundra under Nunavut's midnight sun.
- … and much more!

DUNDURN

VISIT US AT

Dundurn.com
@dundurnpress
Facebook.com/dundurnpress
Pinterest.com/dundurnpress